Strategic Planning
UNLEASHED

An Applied Methodology and Toolkit

By
Ronald J. Recardo and Tim Toterhi

Although the author and publisher have made every effort to ensure that the information in this book was correct at press time, the author and publisher do not assume and hereby disclaim any liability to any party for any loss, damage, or disruption caused by errors or omissions, whether such errors or omissions result from negligence, accident, or any other cause.

TABLE OF CONTENTS

Contents

INTRODUCTION

There is a trend in business today to value style over substance, to promote political savvy over actual innovation – in short, to play it safe. Unfortunately, given the recent economic downturn and the rise of global competition, it's no longer acceptable to tolerate mediocre talent, incremental improvements, or halfhearted attempts at success. Shareholders and stakeholders alike expect and demand more from the companies and business leaders they entrust to get the job done.

Strategic Planning Unleashed takes aim at the often lackluster approach to business fundamentals by providing a no-holds-barred commentary on the core accountabilities of corporate leaders. It provides a realistic, practitioner-oriented approach to business planning, along with the tools to help you get the job done. Whether you're a seasoned C-suite executive or a corporate newbie with a desire to make a difference, this will help you improve performance while building hard-to-acquire internal capability.

WHY ANOTHER BOOK ON STRATEGIC PLANNING?

Most books on this topic focus solely on theoretical frameworks and conceptual models, take a purely academic view of the subject, or rely on an approach endorsed by a single "ideal" company. While this has some value, generic models and classroom-inspired case studies rarely hold up to the rigors of the real world. And though it's true that some companies have obtained success in strategic planning, there is no guarantee that their approach will work for your organization – there is no silver bullet!

Many business leaders have learned the hard way that simply bolting on another company's approach to a problem can be a costly, time-consuming, and often fruitless endeavor. Just look at the waste, frustration, and negative ROI generated by copycat leaders who tried to mirror GE's Workout process or Wal-Mart's supply-chain methodology. Without the right recipe and similar market conditions, you could find yourself cooking with salt instead of sugar.

What makes *Strategic Planning Unleashed* unique is that it was not developed by academics with little business experience. Rather, it has been crafted by seasoned practitioners who have applied the tools in a variety of real-world corporate settings. In addition, the methodology is scalable to organizations of different sizes. The content is not a repackaging of materials already in the public domain but represents new processes, methodologies and insights. The playbook was developed from research projects sponsored by The Catalyst Consulting Group, LLC on strategy development and execution. It includes best practices for strategic planning, and incorporates lessons from the more than two hundred client companies our consultants have worked with over the years.

Regardless of your company's size, complexity, offering portfolio, or geographic scope, this methodology will help your organization analyze its external environment, reach consensus on your sources of competitive advantage, and identify a business strategy and execute it to completion.

WHY STRATEGIC PLANNING FAILS

Any undergrad business major can intuitively point to the need for strategic planning. Organizations have limited resources, so establishing a plan for what needs to be done, by whom, and when, given a series of internal and external realities and constraints, only makes sense if goals are to be achieved and stakeholders satisfied.

For many of us, the strategic-planning process has historically been akin to a black hole. Meetings occur, informal discussions take place, and then, somehow, magic happens – a three-ring binder appears, supposedly summarizing the decisions agreed to by the leadership team. Unfortunately, that's typically where the magic ends. More often than not, the document is rarely reviewed, seldom consulted, and is left to languish on a shelf till next year.

Our research and experience suggest there are six key reasons why strategic planning most often fails.

1. **Too much time is spent on the fluff:** We are not aware of any company that has achieved competitive advantage by having the best-written vision and mission statements! These strategic-planning deliverables are most important when an organization is at a crossroads and needs to do something very different. However, this is not usually the case and a subtle adjustment is often all that is required.

2. **Strategic planning is episodic:** Too often leaders focus primarily on creating a book, which due to a lack of follow through, is ultimately left to collect dust on the shelf. Strategy planning will fail if it is a one-off event built from a series of discontented actions. To be successful, a completed plan must be designed via holistic inputs and properly deployed in the organization.

3. **The process is too complex:** The sophistication of the process must be aligned with the culture, size, and sophistication of the organization.

4. **Not linked to other related systems:** Think of strategic planning as a chain with multiple links. The companies that are acknowledged as being world class at strategic planning have tightly aligned all of the links (inputs and outputs). Depending on the sophistication of your organization, your strategic planning process may need to be aligned with several other systems, including financial forecasting, budgeting, management reporting, HR practices, and human capital planning.

5. **Process is not data driven:** Well-designed strategic-planning processes start with the questions you want to answer or the decisions you want to make. Success is enhanced by collecting the right data in the right format to address those issues.

6. **Poor execution:** Numerous case studies, books, and articles point to organizations that had a great strategic plan but failed miserably because they lacked the leadership, metrics, program management, and change management capabilities to ensure successful rollout. Even the best-designed plan is useless if not properly implemented.

AN OVERVIEW OF THE METHODOLOGY

Let's face it. This is a business book geared toward business people. Your time is valuable and in short supply. So before we do anything else, we want to give you a clear reason for reading this work.

Strategic Planning Unleashed is organized into the following four phases, as noted in **Figure 1** below:

- **Phase 1:** Environmental Assessment
- **Phase 2:** Internal Capabilities Assessment
- **Phase 3:** Strategy Development
- **Phase 4:** Strategy Deployment

Overall Strategic Planning Roadmap

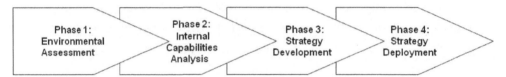

The upcoming sections feature detailed flowcharts of each phase of the strategic planning process. As you view them, keep the following guidelines in mind:

•Highlighted boxes depict a *functional* strategic planning pathway (the "must dos" regardless of the size or scope of your planning initiative)

•Complete the entire pathway for *enterprise-wide* planning

•Each phase includes a series of **Tools** which are mapped *numerically* to activities where they are most commonly used

•Each phase includes a series of **Deliverables** which are mapped *alphabetically* to activities where they are most commonly used

Figure 1: Four Phases of Strategic Planning

We will provide a description of each phase, detailing its purpose and importance in the overall methodology. To ensure you can implement the process in your organization we will also provide the following for each activity:

- Activity purpose and description
- Tasks required to accomplish the activity
- Common tools associated with the tasks – including sample templates and detailed descriptions of each
- Expected deliverables

Although we provide a well-thought-out sequencing of activities based on strategic-planning best practices, the approach is highly flexible and can be customized to the needs of your organization. Furthermore, you will notice that some boxes are highlighted in each phase. These represent the "critical path" – items that should be completed regardless of the size or sophistication of the organization. We chose this design to ensure that the model is scalable and to help practitioners achieve the quickest route to strategy development and deployment.

ADDITIONAL SUPPORT

In our e-book, *Fast Cycle Strategic Planning: An Applied Playbook*, we provided an overview for completing the strategic-planning process – *the What*. This book builds on that work including both the methodology and the tools you should use to execute activities in that process – *the How*.

These assessment instruments, design templates, and implementation tools combine quantitative and qualitative analysis to enhance the probability of success in achieving your business planning targets. If you want assistance in designing a customized strategic-planning process or in developing your strategic plan, or would like more information on training your internal staff to manage the process, please contact us at:

The Catalyst Consulting Group, LLC
Office: (860) 518-3585
www.catalystconsultinggroup.org

PHASE 1: ENVIRONMENTAL ANALYSIS

PURPOSE

Understanding the external environment is a key element of the strategic planning process and one that is often glossed over by time-crunched executives. While many will take time to consider the actions and interests of competitors and customers, other factors are often given only cursory consideration. **Figure 2** below illustrates the various activities required for performing a comprehensive environmental analysis.

Phase 1: Environmental Analysis

Tools:
1. Competitor Summary Template
2. Competitor Assessment Template
3. Competitor Analysis Matrix
4. Customer Prioritization Matrix
5. Product/Buyer Matrix
6. Market Segmentation Template
7. Five Forces Assessment Template
8. Opportunity/Threats Priority Matrix
9. Key Success Factors (KSF) Analysis Matrix

Deliverables:
A. Competitor Analysis Summary
B. Customer Analysis Summary
C. Industry Analysis Summary
D. Strategic Forces Summary
E. Opportunity & Threat Analysis Summary
F. Stakeholder Analysis Summary
G. Environmental & Demographic Trends Analysis Summary
H. Prioritized Opportunity List
I. Prioritized Threats List
J. Key Success Factor Summary

Figure 2: Strategic Planning Phase 1 – Environmental Analysis

In the broadest sense, this phase calls for obtaining a realistic perspective on what is happening outside of the organization that can have a profound impact on the company's success. It involves collecting data on your current and potential

6

competitors and their respective sources of competitive advantage.

A detailed review should also be completed on your **customers**. Elements of this analysis typically include various segmentation strategies, their purchase-decision criteria/desired product/service attributes, which customers are most/least profitable, and most important, a review of their unmet needs.

It's also important to undertake a thorough analysis of the **industry/markets** – a critical step skipped by many senior leaders. You must understand the size of each market, its growth rate, and its profitability. Depending on the size and sophistication of your organization, it may also be necessary to look at other external variables, such as a **geopolitical** and **stakeholder** analysis, which could include your suppliers, channel partners, and unions.

During the environmental scan all present and future opportunities and threats should be identified and prioritized. An **opportunity** is defined as something happening outside of the organization that enhances its ability to compete. These can include:

- Deregulation
- New technology
- Competitor going bankrupt

Conversely, a **threat** is defined as something happening outside of the organization that impedes an organization's ability to compete. These can include:

- New government regulation
- Political instability in an applicable country
- Rising energy costs

Data for Phase 1 can be collected through the following sources:

- US Census data
- Competitor product brochures
- Annual reports/10k's
- Advertisements
- Employees of past competitors
- Suppliers/distributors/channel partners
- Trade/industry groups
- Professional associations
- Third-party data aggregators
- Wall Street analysis

- Patent records
- Speeches by management
- Articles
- Financial filings

TOOLS AND DELIVERABLES

Figure 2 also references the expected deliverables from Phase 1, as well as the tools that enable their development. A deliverable is a tangible work product, such as a summary of a competitor's product and service mix, financials, an updated vision statement, or a balanced scorecard. The key deliverables during this part of the strategic planning process are a summary and prioritization of the opportunities and threats, as well as obtaining consensus across the senior leadership team as to your key success factors.

To enhance the chances of your success, be sure to do a thorough analysis of the competitive landscape, including non-traditional competitors. Specifically:

- Make time to understand your competitors' cost structure and process hierarchy. This will help identify specific areas of weakness and vulnerability that are ripe for attack.
- Identify "disruptive technologies" that can allow you to leapfrog your competitors or that offer threats to your organization.

While all areas of the environmental analysis are important, understanding and actively pursuing ways to best your competition (or make them irrelevant via blue ocean strategies) is a key aspect of Phase 1.

WHO IS ACCOUNTABLE?

Too often strategic planning is performed in a vacuum, with leadership taking little input or feedback from other parts of the organization. In order for strategic planning to be effective a comprehensive source of data points and perspectives should be considered. This is not to advocate a bottom-up approach to strategic planning; the average employee or mid-level manager lacks the line of sight necessary to help shape the strategic direction of a company five years out. However, thoughts from functional, geographically strategic, and business-line leadership should be taken into consideration.

Writing by committee is a nightmare. One individual must have overall responsibility for developing and executing the business strategy. For most small-cap companies, that is the president or business owner. As companies grow and become more complex it may be necessary to hire individuals with specialized experience, such as a vice president of strategic planning. In other cases business planning is decentralized to the SBUs. In this latter scenario, general managers are responsible for planning, and utilize a compact strategic planning task force that is charged with crafting the document. In either case, it is important to include inputs from the following sources:

- Sales/Marketing – for customer insight and input
- Operations/Supply Chain – for product and service-delivery expectations
- Strategic HR – for key talent needs aligned to group
- IT – for infrastructure requirements
- Finance – for a realistic assessment of how to obtain/manage the financial fuel to make it happen

ACTIVITY 1.1: COMPLETE COMPETITOR ANALYSIS

WHAT IS IT?

A competitor analysis is a method of identifying all current and potential competitors. This is a challenging process because, in today's complex, matrix-oriented business environment, they can emerge from a variety of sources, including:

- Suppliers who vertically integrate forward
- Companies that provide similar offerings but in different markets/geographies
- Customers who vertically integrate backward
- Traditional competitors seeking to gain market share or industry influence

To ensure a comprehensive view, leaders must collect data from a myriad of sources, from Wall Street analysts and employees of competitors to trade groups and professional associations.

Performing this step will provide valuable competitor insight. Specifically, the activity will highlight:

- Which competitors present the greatest threat
- Their historical performance and capabilities
- If/where they can be successfully attacked

Analyzing these factors will help determine the relative aggressiveness and focus of your strategic plan – whether you should spend more time in an offensive or defensive posture, or whether, given the additional inputs to follow, you should strive to make the competition irrelevant.

TASKS

Completing the following will help you secure the greatest benefit from your competitor analysis.

1. Identify current competitors

Consider your traditional and nontraditional competitors in terms of the following elements:

- Strategy mix
- Product/service mix
- Positioning
- Product life cycles (opportunity to attack a competitor if it is heavily dependent on products in declining stage)
- Locations of their operations
- Sales channels used: e.g., direct-sales force, wholesalers, distributors
- Buyers
- Geographies/markets served
- Pricing
- Strengths/weaknesses

Cost structure (number of employees, direct labor, overhead – do they have an advantage?)

2. Review your key competitors' value chain

Conduct a data-based comparison of your capabilities vs. those of your competitors and then ask yourself the following:

- Where are they vulnerable?
- Where do they have an advantage and why?
- Are there any lessons from competitors that you can incorporate into your own organization?

3. Assess your competitors' overall position

Build on step two by contrasting your company's position vs. your competitors' by asking the following questions:

- What have competitors done that has succeeded or failed?
- Can any weak competitors be induced to exit the marketplace?
- Are there opportunities for acquiring any undervalued competitors?
- What are your competitors' likely strategic thrusts and how should your organization respond?
- Does any party have a distinct cost advantage?
- What is the market segmentation?
- What are the comparative overall sales, sales by market, and product/service sales?

4. Assess competitors' financial trends

Take time to analyze the financial position of your competitors. Typically, a midterm analysis or the past three years is a reasonable timeframe to assess. To be effective, include the following in your review where possible:

- Net income
- Cash flow
- Net income/sales
- Gross profit/sales
- Operating profit/sales
- ROA, ROI, ROE

5. Identify potential competitors

Having completed this assessment, reevaluate the actual competitive landscape.

Your review may highlight new competitive forces or indicate that one-time rivals have stumbled and lost market dominance. Regardless of competitor type or status, consider the following:

- Who are they?
- What is their likely strategy?
- What are their sources of competitive advantage?
- What markets are they most likely to enter?

Remember to include:

- Companies that cross industries/markets
- Companies that take on forward/backward vertical integration

6. Identify trends and implications

Be sure to round out your analysis by identifying competitive trends and the potential implications they may have on your organization.

TOOLS

To ensure you conduct the most comprehensive competitive analysis we have developed the following tools.

PHASE 1, TOOL 1: COMPETITOR SUMMARY TEMPLATE

This provides an executive summary of key competitors across a variety of critical factors. It's important to consider all relevant factors when completing this analysis. Sample variables are noted in the template below, but these can be customized for your industry and expanded to include more detail. For example, you might want to add sections on pricing, technology, or R&D pipeline.

You can also use this tool to rank your competitors in terms of overall organizational capability or a single vital characteristic. Be sure to include atypical or potential competitors in your analysis. Given the speed and complexity of business today, your greatest threat could come from emerging nontraditional players.

Competitiveness Variables	Competitor 1	Competitor 2	Competitor 3	Competitor 4	Competitor 5
History					
Product/service mix					
Markets served					
Locations					
Strengths					
Weaknesses					
Suppliers					
Distribution					

PHASE 1, TOOL 2: COMPETITOR ASSESSMENT TEMPLATE

This provides an assessment of competitors' offerings by a variety of factors during a specified time. This tool enhances your original competitive overview by allowing you to expand the product/service analysis for specific key competitors. It not only enables you to review the effectiveness of each product/service in terms of current market share; it also overlays the relevant financial data associated with the offering to ensure a clearer picture.

Criteria	Year 1	Year 2	Year 3
Product A – Brief Description			
Product B – Brief Description			
Product C – Brief Description			

Criteria	Year 1	Year 2	Year 3
Revenues			
Market Share			
Current Ratio			
Profitability			

PHASE 1, TOOL 3: COMPETITOR ANALYSIS MATRIX

This tool allows you to capture an even greater level of detail. As noted in the example below, the competitor analysis matrix dissects a competitor from both an external vantage point (i.e., its business model, offerings, and market segmentation) as well as various factors associated with an internal assessment. These include a speculative view of the organization's perceived competitive advantages and strengths and weaknesses.

External Analysis			
Competitor/ Business Model	*Annual Revenues*	*Market Segmentation*	*Product/ Service Mix*
J Andrews – Organized by industry and practice area	$172MM	Focus on small & mid-cap	Interim management at C-suite levels, liquidity work, bankruptcy strategy/ preparedness
Astro – Organized by geography and practice area	$690MM	Address all vertical markets above $20MM in revenues	2-sided business with debtor and creditor (AA) services

Internal Analysis				
Competitor/ Business Model	*Competitive Advantages*	*Industry Strengths*	*Weaknesses*	*Notes*
J Andrews – Organized by industry and practice area	Marketing orientation, strong brand, one of the original players in the market, bench strength to complete big projects, perceived to have clout (referrers afraid of losing their referrals), well capitalized	High tech, healthcare	Not involved in operations, comprised of accountants that do financial turnaround – spreadsheet jockeys, highest rate structure, arrogance	Can be attacked by developing relationships with large legal firms, workout functions within banks
Astro – Organized by geography and practice area	Founder came out of workout bank. Have debtor/creditor practice (more predictable revenues, better relationships with referrers)	Biotech, manufacturing, financial services	High overhead, much stronger presence in Europe	Formidable competitor, avoid going head to head in Europe

This comprehensive review allows you to draw certain conclusions (in the notes section) that can indicate your next move in relation to either a specific competitor or the overall competitive landscape.

DELIVERABLE

At the completion of this task you will create the following deliverable that will provide critical input to your overall strategic plan.

A.   Competitor Analysis Summary

Please Note: Strategic planning deliverables are unique to each organization. The format, level of detail, and amount of analytical rigor are based on the specific questions you want to answer or decisions you want to make. Therefore deliverables are considered to be highly proprietary. If you want assistance with compiling this information or general guidance with any part of the strategic-planning process please contact us via **www.catalystconsultinggroup.org**.

ACTIVITY 1.2: COMPLETE CUSTOMER ASSESSMENT

WHAT IS IT?

During this activity an analysis of the customer base is undertaken to understand a number of variables, such as customer segments, who are the desired/undesired customers, and customer's buying criteria. A thorough customer analysis will help an organization understand which customers are mission critical, how to enhance market share and customer satisfaction, and which opportunities will differentiate them from the competition.

TASKS

Completing the following will help you secure the greatest benefit from your customer analysis.

1. Define your market segments

Customers may be categorized by:

- Usage level
- Socio-demographics
- Geography
- Price sensitivity
- Age
- Sex
- Income level

2. Understand the desired product/service attributes by customer segment

Do they vary by market segment? Which ones are unsatisfied? Examples include:

- Price
- Quality
- Functionality
- Service

3. Understand purchaser behavior

- Frequency of purchase
- Average purchase price
- Method – cash or credit
- Motivation – (brand, loyalty, effects of discounts, advertising)

4. Collect additional customer data

- Contact old customers that switched to a competitor to fully understand the underlying reasons
- Contact competitors' customers to understand why they are working with a competitor instead of you

5. Understand demographics of buyers (if applicable)

- Age
- Sex
- Income/family size

- Occupation/education
- Race
- Spending patterns

6. **Understand the profitability of each customer segment**
   - Which customers offer the lowest/highest profitability?
   - Identify percentage of sales by each customer
   - Identify alternative customer segments

7. **Fully understand how each customer uses your product/service**
   - Understand the specific need(s) it fulfills
   - Consider both practical / actual and intangible needs

8. **Understand industry dynamics**
   - Seasonality
   - Cost structure

9. **Assess satisfaction levels**
   - What are the sources of dissatisfaction?
   - Map the sources back to organization architecture, internal capabilities, etc.
   - Which aspects of your product/service or distribution process can cause you to lose business?

10. **Identify unmet needs**
    - This can be helpful in identifying white space i.e. new market areas
    - It can also help highlight sources of differentiation

11. **Identify substitutes**
    Note which products perform the same function as current industry product (e.g., sugar vs. corn syrup, steel vs. aluminum)
    - Who makes these substitute products?
    - What are the barriers to entry?

12. **Identify trends and implications**

13. Begin preliminary analysis
- Should you focus on fewer customers?
- Are you managing the product portfolio?

TOOLS

To ensure you conduct the most comprehensive customer analysis, use the following tool.

PHASE 1, TOOL 4: CUSTOMER PRIORITIZATION MATRIX

This provides a summary of your customer set by a series of strategic factors. In addition to highlighting gaps in your customer portfolio, this tool will help ensure you chase the right business for the right reasons. Too often organizations find themselves at the mercy of a few key customers due to an unhealthy mix or because they're operating solely in the transactional space when their true intention is to offer a higher-level customer value proposition.

One of the most important things an organization can do is be thoughtful about their collective time signature – where and how they spend their resources in pursuit of business victories. While all customers are important, they are not all created equally. An effective strategic plan will take into account the current relationship with each customer (commodity player vs. true strategic partnership) and ensure the balance aligns with future goals.

Customers	Prioritization Criteria			
	Profitability	Strategic Importance	Ease of Doing Business	Other
Customer A				
Customer B				
Customer C				
Customer D				

DELIVERABLE

Completing this step will provide the following input for use in your overall strategic plan.

B. Customer Analysis Summary

ACTIVITY 1.3: COMPLETE INDUSTRY ASSESSMENT

WHAT IS IT?

This activity is extremely important because winning in the marketplace is to a great extent determined by where you place your bets. This activity builds on some of the work completed in the previous activity to ensure all current and potential markets are thoroughly analyzed as a key factor in developing strategic alternatives.

TASKS

Completing the following will help ensure you secure the greatest benefit from your industry assessment.

1. **Understand the current and potential market segments**
   - What are the submarkets?
   - How intense is the competition?
   - What are the alternative distribution channels?

2. **Understand the size of each market segment**
   - Be sure to focus on current realities, not projections or forecasts

3. **Assess the growth rates of each market segment**
   - Understand growth drivers

4. **Assess the profitability of each market segment**
   - Compare market segment growth to industry growth

5. Prioritize current and potential market segments

Define any barriers to entry, such as:

- Patents
- Skill sets
- Capital intensity
- Regulation
- Supply-source control
- Distribution
- Customer loyalty

6. Identify trends and implications

TOOLS

To ensure you conduct the most comprehensive industry assessment, use the following tools.

PHASE 1, TOOL 5: PRODUCT/BUYER MATRIX

This tool is divided into two sections. The first allows you to view the various products/services your organization offers in terms of both the market potential and your company's capabilities in that area. Viewing this will help you draw conclusions on where to place your energy.

Note: this analysis can be expanded to include a comparison of your capabilities to those of your competitors.

PRODUCT OR SERVICE/MARKET MATRIX

Offering	Market Potential	Firm's Capabilities	Notes/Conclusions
Product A	2	1	
Product B	1	2	
Product C	3	3	
Service A	3	2	
Service B	2	1	
Service C	1	3	
See legend next page			

Legend	
Market Potential	**Firm's Capabilities**
Small - 1	Low - 1
Medium - 2	Average - 2
Large - 3	High - 3

The second part of this tool allows you to view the products/services in your industry through a consumer-oriented lens. Specifically, it helps you identify the various stakeholders on the particular buying decisions and weight their respective levels of influence. This analysis, when used in conjunction with the tool above, will help you marshal your best resources toward promoting offerings that have the greatest market potential and buyer appeal, and then leverage that work to target specific needs of the various buying influences you encounter.

Please note that the tool below should be customized to reflect the various stakeholders and nomenclature in your industry. For example, in some industries procurement or strategic sourcing departments may have a high status in the buying process, while in others they could be virtually nonexistent. This tool will be most useful when tailored to the selling realities within your space – another reason to involve a broader group in the strategic plan design.

PRODUCT OR SERVICE – BUYER MATRIX

Offering	Stakeholder Level of influence				
	User	Technical Expert	Executive	Budget Holder	Gatekeeper
Product A	1	2	3	2	2
Product B					
Product C					
Service A					
Service B					
Service C					

Legend: 1- low, 2 = medium, 3 = high level of influence

PHASE 1, TOOL 6: MARKET SEGMENTATION TEMPLATE

The Market Segmentation Template is also useful in completing your industry assessment. The template below illustrates a completed example of this tool, allowing you to map your competitors' (or your own) product/service offerings versus geographies and placement category.

Matching this data to competitive intelligence and consumer demand will help determine both unexploited opportunities and potential market saturation. Seasoned strategists can also use this input to read between the lines and ferret out potential blue ocean opportunities that are currently unaddressed by any player in the space.

Products	Regions			Type of Car			
	North America	South America	Asia Pacific	Luxury	Family	Hybrid	Sport
Cadillac Deville	X	X		X			
Saturn Sky	X				X		
Chevrolet Volt	X		X			X	
Chevrolet Camaro	X						X
Buick Enclave	X	X		X			

DELIVERABLE

Completing this step will provide the following for use in your overall strategic plan.

C. Industry Analysis Summary

ACTIVITY 1.4: COMPLETE SUPPLIER ASSESSMENT

WHAT IS IT?

Supplier power is a function of:

- The number of suppliers in relation to industry needs/supplier concentration
- The size (dollar amount) of purchases relative to overall supplies purchased
- Costs for you to switch to another supplier
- The degree to which the supplier's product is important to your business (substitutability)
- The degree to which their products are differentiated
- The level of difficulty or cost associated with switching vendors
- The potential for forward vertical integration

TASKS

A high-level supplier assessment should address at least the following three tasks:

1. Review the historical performance of your suppliers

Review all available performance data, including:

- Cost
- Performance to schedule
- Quality levels

2. Determine power of suppliers

Supplier power is a function of:

- Number of suppliers
- Number of product substitutes
- Number of customers
- Their specialized skill sets

3. Identify trends and implications

TOOLS

To ensure you conduct the most comprehensive supplier assessment, we recommend the use of the following tool or its equivalent.

PHASE 1, TOOL 7: FIVE FORCES ASSESSMENT TEMPLATE

This tool helps business leaders review strategic variables that impact organizational performance, including suppliers. The variables include:

- **Buyer's Power** – factors that provide the purchasing organization with strategic leverage in negotiations
- **Supplier's Power** – factors that provide the selling organization with strategic leverage in negotiations
- **Rivalry Power** – includes industry-related elements that influence the spread of power between the parties
- **Threat of Product Substitutes** – considers both pricing and customer-loyalty dynamics that affect the relationship
- **Threat of New Entrants** – considers factors related to increasing traditional and nontraditional competitive forces that can shift the buyer–supplier power dynamic

Buyer's Power – Variables	Key	High	Medium	Low
Percentage of industry output purchased by the buyer	The larger the volumes, the **higher** the power			
Buyer has low switching cost or has many competitors to choose from	The lower the switching costs or the greater the number of competitors to choose from, the **higher** the buyer power			
Product cost as a percentage of the cost of the buyer group's output	The higher the cost percentage, the **lower** the power			

Buyer's Power – Variables	Key	High	Medium	Low
The number of substitute products	The larger the number of substitute products, the **higher** the power			
Degree of product customization	The higher the customization, the **higher** the buyer power			

Supplier's Power – Variables	Key	High	Medium	Low
Number of suppliers	The fewer the suppliers, the **higher** their power			
Number of product substitutes	The fewer the substitutes, the **higher** the supplier power			
Number of customers	A supplier who has a large customer base, with no customers generating a disproportionate percentage of revenue, has **high** supplier power			
Specialized skill sets	When the buyer has a strong need for suppliers' skills, the supplier has **high** power			

Rivalry Power – Variables	Key	High	Medium	Low
Industry growth rates	If growth is slow, growth comes from taking customers away from the competition, thus the **higher** the rivalry			
Exit barriers	The higher the exit barriers, the **higher** the rivalry			
Number of customers	The smaller the customer-base the **higher** rivalry			

Threat of Substitute Products – Variables	Key	High	Medium	Low
Price/performance compared to existing product	If price is lower and/or performance functionality is better, threat of substitution is **high**			
Switching costs	The lower the switching cost, the **higher** the threat of substitution			
Buyer propensity to substitute	If the buyer has limited customer loyalty, the **higher** the threat of substitution			

Threat of New Entrants – *Variables*	Key	High	Medium	Low
Capital intensity	If there are low capitalization requirements, the threat of a new entrant is **higher**			
Expected retaliation	If the probability of retaliation is low, the threat of a new entrant is **higher**			
Degree of brand identify	If there is limited brand strength, the threat of a new entrant is **higher**			
Product distribution	The easier it is to get access to distribution, the **higher** the threat of a new entrant			
Buyer propensity to substitute	If the buyer has limited customer loyalty, the **higher** the threat of substitution			

DELIVERABLE

Completing this step will provide the following for use in your overall strategic plan:

D. Strategic Forces Summary

ACTIVITY 1.5: COMPLETE GEOPOLITICAL ANALYSIS

WHAT IS IT?

This activity is more important for organizations that compete globally. During this activity it is important to fully understand the specific variables that impact your organization's performance, such as exchange rates, political instability in a given country, and supply chains.

TASKS

Completing the following will help ensure you secure the greatest benefit from your geopolitical analysis.

1. **Identify the specific geopolitical variables that affect the organization**
   Examples include:
   - New laws/regulation
   - Changes in political leadership
   - Tax or incentive changes
   - Currency fluctuations
   - Political instability

2. **Determine how to collect this information**
   There are a variety of ways to approach data gathering. The more sources selected, the more comprehensive the data set. However, more is not always better. Be careful not to become overwhelmed by the collection process.

3. **Analyze the data to identify trends and implications**

4. **Draw conclusions from your research**

TOOLS

To ensure you conduct the most comprehensive supplier assessment we recommend the use of the following tool or its equivalent.

PHASE 1, TOOL 8: OPPORTUNITY/THREAT PRIORITY MATRIX

This tool is helpful in prioritizing the opportunities and threats in the external environment. An analysis that includes the external forces of competitors, customers, and suppliers is incomplete without a thorough understanding of the wider geopolitical landscape in which the business operates. This is particularly important for global organizations that can be affected by the complex, often fast-paced changes wrought by political realities in foreign countries.

The opportunity/threat priority matrix tool will help you gain a greater understanding of the external forces that could disrupt or enhance your strategic efforts. Use the following steps to complete this exercise:

- Identify all opportunities and threats in column 1
- For each opportunity/threat, place an "I" in the column that most corresponds to the perceived level of **impact**, from low to high
- For each opportunity/threat, place an "P" in the column that most corresponds to the perceived level of **probability** of occurrence, from low to high

Opportunities & Threats	Probability & Impact Assessment				
	Low	Medium-low	Average	Medium-high	High
I. Opportunities					
# 1					
# 2					
# 3					
# 4					
# 5					

Opportunities & Threats	Probability & Impact Assessment				
	Low	Medium-low	Average	Medium-high	High
II. Threats					
# 1					
# 2					
# 3					
# 4					
# 5					

DELIVERABLE

Completing this step will provide the following for use in your overall strategic plan.

E. Opportunity and Threat Analysis Summary

ACTIVITY 1.6: COMPLETE STAKEHOLDER ANALYSIS

WHAT IS IT?

There are a number of stakeholders to be concerned about when undertaking a strategic planning process. It is important to understand the relative strength of each. If applicable, pay careful attention to the stakeholders closest to the center of your value chain.

TASKS

Completing the following will help you secure the greatest benefit from your stakeholder analysis.

1. Brainstorm the key organizational stakeholders

Be sure to look beyond the usual suspects to compile a comprehensive list. Players can include:

- Stockholders
- Unions
- Suppliers
- Channel partners
- Internal parties such as employees, unions, managers, and leadership

2. Assess the strength of each stakeholder group

3. Assess the historical relationships with each stakeholder group

4. Identify the preliminary issues you will need to address to successfully engage each stakeholder group

5. Identify trends and implications

TOOLS

The Opportunity/Threat Priority Matrix discussed in Activity 1.5 can also be helpful in this stage of the analysis.

DELIVERABLE

Completing this step will provide the following for use in your overall strategic plan.

F. Stakeholder Analysis Summary

ACTIVITY 1.7: COMPLETE ECONOMIC AND DEMOGRAPHIC ANALYSIS

WHAT IS IT?

Depending on the size and type of organization, it can be heavily impacted by any number of economic and/or demographic trends. It is important to understand these trends, identify how they are likely to impact the organization, and note underlying assumptions.

KEY TASKS

Completing the following will help you secure the greatest benefit from your economic and demographic analysis.

1. Identify economic variables that are likely to impact the organization

Examples include:

- Inflation rates
- Interest rates
- Energy costs
- Unemployment rates
- Currency fluctuations

2. Identify demographic trends that are likely to impact the organization

Examples include:

- Age distribution
- Geographic shifts
- Socioeconomic trends
- Changes in buyer values
- Changes in lifestyle

3. Identify trends and implications

TOOLS

Since most organizations have a proprietary means or preferred method of collecting this information, we have not provided a standalone tool for this activity. However, the Opportunity/Threat Priority Matrix discussed in Activity 1.5 can also be helpful in this stage of the analysis.

DELIVERABLE

Completing this step will provide the following for use in your overall strategic plan.

G. Environmental and Demographic Trends Analysis Summary

This deliverable should summarize cause and effect between economic and demographic variables and organizational performance. It should also include a forecast of these changes and its underlying assumptions.

ACTIVITY 1.8: IDENTIFY OPPORTUNITIES

WHAT IS IT?

An opportunity is something happening outside of the organization that **enhances** its ability to compete. Examples include:

- Deregulation
- New technology
- Competitor going bankrupt

TASKS

Completing the following will help you secure the greatest benefit from your analysis of potential opportunities.

1. **Use all of the data collected during Phase 1 to identify opportunities**

2. **Prioritize each opportunity according to:**
   - Probability of occurrence
   - Degree of impact

3. For the "critical few" opportunities, assess whether the organization can impact them

4. Identify potential strategic alternatives

TOOLS

The Opportunity/Threat Priority Matrix discussed in Activity 1.5 can also be helpful in this stage of the analysis.

DELIVERABLE

H. Prioritized Opportunities List

ACTIVITY 1.9: IDENTIFY THREATS

WHAT IS IT?

A threat is something happening outside of the organization that **threatens** its ability to compete. Examples include:
- New government regulation
- Political instability in a country where you do business
- Rising energy costs

TASKS

Completing the following will help ensure you secure the greatest benefit from your analysis of potential threats.

1. Use all the data collected during this phase to identify threats such as disruptive technologies

2. Prioritize each threat according to:
- Probability of occurrence
- Degree of impact

3. For the "critical few" threats, assess whether the organization can impact them

4. Identify potential strategic alternatives

TOOLS

The Opportunity/Threat Priority Matrix discussed in Activity 1.5 can also be helpful in this stage of the analysis.

DELIVERABLE

Completing this step will provide the following for use in your overall strategic plan.

I. Prioritized Threats List

ACTIVITY 1.10: DETERMINE KEY SUCCESS FACTORS

WHAT IS IT?

Key success factors (KSF) are defined as those variables that you must excel at to be successful. KSF allow an organization to assess their capabilities in relationship to the marketplace and assess their capabilities vis-à-vis competitors. Examples of KSF include:

- Geographic location
- Relationships with customers
- Distribution channel
- New product innovation
- Price
- Delivery
- Quick response to market change

- Product availability
- Brand recognition

TASKS
The following tasks are instrumental in determining your KSF.

1. Review industry trends

2. Identify the most successful industry competitors

3. Compare the capabilities of the most successful companies to average and below-average performers
Be sure to assess:
- Value chain
- Product/service offerings

4. Compare organization performance relative to each KSF
For example, if the customer values low cost, the KSF may be low inventory of raw/finished goods, high labor productivity, low cost facilities, and/or low labor cost.

5. Compare competitor performance relative to each KSF

6. Identify sources of differentiation

TOOLS
To ensure you conduct the most comprehensive competitive analysis, use the following tool.

PHASE 1, TOOL 9: KSF ANALYSIS MATRIX
This tool will help you list and rank the importance of KSF in your space in terms of both the buyer's view and market realities: e.g., the collective customer pool values attribute X and the leading competitors in the space excel at that

dimension as a component of securing the top spot. This tool also enables you to list your organization's current ability in that specific KSF. Analyzing the results of this assessment will help you make decisions on where to place your focus to improve your standings.

	Key Success Factors	Rank	(5=Outstanding, 3=Average, 1=Minimal)				
1)			5	4	3	2	1
2)			5	4	3	2	1
3)			5	4	3	2	1
4)			5	4	3	2	1
5)			5	4	3	2	1
6)			5	4	3	2	1
7)			5	4	3	2	1
8)			5	4	3	2	1

DELIVERABLE:

Completing this step will provide the following for use in your overall strategic plan.

J.   Key Success Factors (KSF) Summary

PHASE 2: INTERNAL CAPABILITIES ANALYSIS

PURPOSE

While understanding the external forces that shape your industry's landscape is a key component of the strategic plan, obtaining a realistic and unbiased view of your internal capabilities is just as critical. The primary objective in Phase 2 is to help leaders shift their focus from an external lens, which is concerned with industry-wide issues, economic and geo-political concerns, and overall market dynamics, to an internal lens, which is concerned with self-examination. History is littered with the wrecks of companies that went after a viable market opportunity but did not have the internal capabilities to successfully capture it.

Looking inward and taking stock of your organization's core capabilities and associated strengths and weaknesses can be a difficult task. While there are a variety of reasons why leaders have trouble with this phase, the most common relate to a series of faulty leadership assumptions. These include:

- Key stakeholders already understand their organization
- Research time is better allocated elsewhere
- Biases and blind spots do not exist
- Employees, managers, and junior leaders don't filter negative perceptions when communicating up the chain of command

These assumptions, coupled with the rarely discussed reality that many leaders are afraid of uncovering "the ugly truth," often result in this phase being skipped or performed in a superficial manner. Unfortunately, if you want develop competitive advantage you must be brave enough to confront the brutal facts and see the true "as-is" state of your organization. This view will provide a healthy sanity check on your capabilities and provide clues as to which opportunities can be capitalized on, which threats should be avoided, and which risks should be mitigated at all costs.

Too often, leaders who lack a realistic assessment of their organizations spend precious resources chasing the wrong opportunities. Though these wins may be captured in theory, they are often unattainable because the organization lacks the necessary assets, core capabilities, appropriate culture, and/or business model. In today's competitive world, knowing what markets to chase can often spell the difference between world-class performance and bankruptcy.

Figure 3 below illustrates the various activities required for performing a comprehensive internal capabilities analysis.

Phase 2: Internal Capabilities Analysis

Tools:
1. Value Chain Analysis
2. Process Hierarchy Template
3. Historical Financial Analysis Template
4. Product/Service Attributes vs. Internal Capabilities Worksheet
5. Capabilities vs. Importance Matrix
6. Competitive Assessment Table

Deliverables:
A. Technology Architecture Summary
B. Organization Architecture Summary
C. Process Architecture Summary
D. Financial Analysis (company vs. competitors) Summary
E. Summary of Strengths
F. Summary of Weaknesses
G. Sources of Competitive Advantage

Figure 3: Strategic Planning Phase 2 –Internal Capabilities Analysis

Please Note: As shown in Figure 3, completing each activity is made easier through the use of the noted tools. In addition, we have mapped where deliverables are commonly created.

To help you navigate the complexities of the internal assessment, we have developed a framework called the **TOPS Model** to describe the architecture present within all organizations. It is comprised of three components: **T**echnology, **O**rganization, and **P**rocess.

TOPS Model

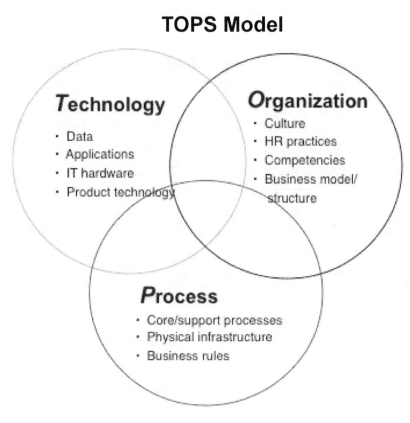

Figure 4: TOPS Model

As you can see in Figure 4 above, these elements are interrelated and dependent on one another to drive success in an organization. An integral component of the strategic-planning process is being able to understand your current capability in each area while evaluating what will be needed in the future. Additionally, it is important to be able to identify your internal strengths and weaknesses.

Assessing your organization using this framework will provide a variety of findings, including areas of strength to leverage, weaknesses to shore up, and elements that are adequately performed but may benefit from a mild investment/process enhancement. Use this model as a guide as you work through the various tasks associated with the internal capabilities study.

TOOLS AND DELIVERABLES

Figure 3 above also references the expected deliverables from Phase 2 as well as the tools that enable their development. The key deliverables during this part of the strategic planning process are a summary of your company's capabilities with specific attention placed on process, technology, and organizational elements as well as the overall financial health. These items can illustrate your strengths and weakness, painting a picture of your sources of competitive advantage.

Also, to expedite your success in this phase be sure to do the following:

- Obtain consensus across the executive team on your sources of competitive advantage. Never shortchange these areas in terms of resourcing and budgeting.
- Have a candid conversation about and agree on your actual core capabilities. Remember, just because there is a market opportunity doesn't mean you have the ability to successfully take advantage of it. Most strategies and market opportunities require certain core capabilities. If you don't have them you will not be successful in chasing an external opportunity.

WHO IS ACCOUNTABLE?

It is important to involve a diverse, cross-functional taskforce for this phase of the strategic planning process. While having inputs from various parties on the external view is helpful, it is critical when considering internal capabilities. We won't repeat the recommended areas of inclusion noted in Phase 1. We will however, point out that the criteria used to select participants from those disciplines is vital to success.

To ensure you select the best possible stakeholder participants, be sure to look for the following:

- Deep understanding of the company, as well as the function/department and its capabilities
- Strength of conviction – ability to speak honestly and point out weaknesses, even if politically charged
- Respected – must have enough organizational clout to be taken seriously

ACTIVITY 2.1: ASSESS TECHNOLOGY ARCHITECTURE

WHAT IS IT?

The technology architecture is comprised of:

- Data (what is stored, where it is stored, who has access, etc.)
- Applications (software)
- IT hardware
- Product technology (the technology that delivers the core product/service)

Technology capability is either a gate-limiting factor or a strength that can allow you to capture market opportunities.

TASKS

Completing the following will help you secure the greatest benefit from your technology architecture assessment.

1. Catalog and evaluate your technology assets

2. Compare the organization's capability to best practices, benchmarks, and competitors' capabilities

3. Assess historical performance/capability and the implications that environmental demands have on the technology architecture

4. Identify strengths and weaknesses

TOOLS

To ensure you conduct the most comprehensive analysis of this element, use the following tool.

PHASE 2, TOOL 1: VALUE CHAIN ANALYSIS

A value chain is a visual representation of the processes and activities an organization completes to deliver its products and services. This tool can be used to:

- Fully understand how an organization creates value from each activity
- See the costs associated with each activity
- Identify where and how integration targets can be realized
- Identify sources of competitive advantage

The elements of the value chain are separated into *primary* and *support* processes, all of which should add value to the product or service produced.

The *primary* processes are those activities that directly produce the product or service and include:

- Inbound Logistics
- Operations
- Outbound Logistics
- Marketing and Sales
- Service

The *support* processes are those activities that facilitate the primary processes and include:

- Organizational Infrastructure
- HRM
- Technology Development
- Procurement

It is important to remember that the creation of a value chain is labor/data intensive and is an iterative process. This tool is by far the most sophisticated in the strategic planning toolbox and may require partnering with a person who has used it before. The following steps should prove useful in your design:

Determine the scope and level of detail of the value chain

A value chain can be completed exclusively for your operations business or it could be widened to incorporate your suppliers' and channel partners' value chains creating an overall business value chain. It can also be quite advantageous to develop a value chain for your key competitors to compare and contrast capabilities, costs, and sources of competitive advantage.

Develop the selected value chain

Identify activities and then assign them to the most appropriate part of the value chain. Establish the basic framework of the value chain by identifying the principal activities of the organization. Refer to relevant data sources such as process documentation and organization structure charts. Data can also be collected from interviews, surveys, targeted workshops, benchmarking, and secondary research. The key is to fully understand the hierarchy of processes involved in transforming inputs into outputs that are delivered to your customers. The development of a value chain is similar to documenting a process. Key considerations include:

- Thoroughly understanding the purpose of each process/activity
- Ordering the activities
- Understanding the cost drivers
- Understanding the differences in the way competitors perform key activities. This can assist in identifying improvement opportunities, ideas for improving performance, and sources of competitive advantage

Sample of a Generic Value Chain

Value chain analysis allows you to visually depict your capabilities vs. competitors'

Inbound Logistics	Operations	Outbound Logistics	Customer Service	Marketing & Sales
Organization Infrastructure				
Human Resource Management				
Technology Development				
Procurement				

Establish the relative importance of different activities in the total cost of the products and services you deliver.

Use Activity Based Costing to assign operating costs and assets to each value activity. Even without such detailed cost data, you can identify the critical activities, establish which activities are performed relatively efficiently, identify cost drivers, and offer recommendations.

Compare costs by activity

To establish which activities the organization performs relatively efficiently and which it does not, benchmark unit costs for each activity against those of competitors and other world-class organizations. It is also important to identify which activities are non-value-added and assess whether the process can be modified to improve the ratio of value to non-value activities.

Identify cost drivers

These will vary by industry and company. For example, the cost drivers of manufacturing can include the number of plants, their throughput, the number of products, compensation levels, and capacity/utilization levels.

Expand on the value chains

Seek opportunities for overall optimization of activities throughout the value chain, which may lead to cost reduction and/or speed, quality, or efficiency enhancements.

- **Example 1:** Consolidating purchase orders to increase discounts increases inventories.
- **Example 2:** High-quality parts and materials reduce costs of defects at later stages.
- **Example 3:** Designing different models around common components and platforms reduces manufacturing costs

It is likely that the value chain will need to be documented at different levels of detail to illustrate key lessons (See samples below).

Sample Value Chain

	INBOUND LOGISTICS	OPERATIONS	OUTBOUND LOGISTICS	MKTG. & SALES	SERVICE
FIRM INFRASTRUCTURE	TOP MANAGEMENT SUPPORT IN SELLING FACILITIES THAT ENHANCE THE FIRM'S IMAGE SUPERIOR MANAGEMENT INFORMATION SYSTEM				
HUMAN RESOURCE MANAGEMENT	Strong Management Development Program	Stable Workforce Quality of Work Life Programs Program to attract the Best Scientists and Engineers		Sales Incentives to retain Best Salesperson Recruiting better Qualified Sales and Service Personnel	Executive Training of Service Technicians
TECHNOLOGY DEVELOPMENT	Superior Material Handling & Sorting Technology Proprietary Quality Assurance Equipment	Unique Product Features Rapid Model Introductions Unique Production Process of Machines Automated Inspection Procedures	Unique Vehicle Scheduling Software Special Purpose Vehicles or Containers	Applications Engineering Support Superior Media Research Most Rapid Quotations for Tailored Models	Advanced Servicing Techniques
PROCUREMENT	Most Reliable Transportation for Inbound Deliveries	Highest Quality Incoming Raw Mtrl probs Highest Quality Components	Best Located Warehouses Transportation Suppliers that Minimize Damage	Most Desirable Media Placements Product Positioning and Image	Problems with Quality Replacement Parts
	Handling of Inputs that Minimizes Damage or Degradation Timelines of Supply to the Manufacturing Process	Supplier certification Utilization of WCM Process redesign Flexible manufacturing Including JIT	Rapid and Timely Delivery Accurate and Responsive Order Processing Handling that Minimizes Damage	High Advertising Level and Quality High Sales Force Coverage and Quality Personal Relationships with Channels of Buyers Superior Technical Literature & Other Sales Aides Most Extensive Promotion Most Extensive Credit to Buyers or Channels	Rapid Installation High Service Quality Complete Field Stocking of Replacement Parts Wide Service Coverage Extensive Buyer Training

MARGIN

47

Sample Value Chain

Analyze the value chain

- Identify cross-linkages between value chains (competitors, suppliers, channel partners) as areas for potential synergy that could lead to cost reduction, speed, quality, or efficiency enhancements.

- Identify opportunities to reduce costs and increase efficiencies (or whatever your strategic objective is). By identifying areas of comparative inefficiency and the cost drivers for each, opportunities for cost reduction and efficiency improvement become evident. Determine whether they are still needed, and then examine ways of improving efficiency and trying to achieve cost reductions to increase the profit margins for the business.

- Decide which value chain functions/ processes to integrate and use activity based costing (ABC) to help identify potential opportunities for cost reduction.

DELIVERABLE

Completing this step will provide the following for use in your strategic plan:

A. Technology Architecture Summary

ACTIVITY 2.2: ASSESS ORGANIZATION ARCHITECTURE

WHAT IS IT?

The organization architecture is comprised of the following elements:

- Business systems such as planning and budgeting
- Human resource practices/policies such as recruiting, benefits, compensation, talent management, training, etc.
- Capabilities and workforce competencies
- Organization structural elements such as job design, reporting relationships, staffing levels

Aligning organization architecture is a critical component for successful strategy deployment.

TASKS

Completing the following will help you secure the greatest benefit from your organization architecture assessment.

1. **Catalog and evaluate the components of your organization architecture**
   - Identify existing data inputs such as management reports, internal/external customer feedback, and staff input that can be used to assess each component of organization architecture
   - Identify information gaps and determine how you will collect any key missing information

2. **Compare the organization's capability to best practices, benchmarks, and competitors' capabilities**

3. **Assess historical performance/capability and the implications environmental demands have on the organization architecture**

4. **Identify strengths/weaknesses**

TOOLS

The Value Chain Analysis discussed in Activity 2.1 can also be helpful in this stage of the process.

DELIVERABLE

Completing this step will provide the following for use in your overall strategic plan:

B. Organization Architecture Summary

ACTIVITY 2.3: ASSESS PROCESS ARCHITECTURE

WHAT IS IT?

The process architecture is composed of the following elements:
- Administrative policies or business rules that drive behavior
- Business processes
- Physical infrastructure of the business, including site strategy, number and location of work locations, etc.
- Physical layout of work areas: e.g., the arrangement of offices and conference rooms

The process architecture represents how work gets done as it flows across the organization and its physical assets. Strategy deployment is deeply influenced by these core and support processes.

TASKS

Completing the following will help you secure the greatest benefit from your process architecture assessment.

1. **Catalog your core and support processes**

2. **Evaluate the capability of these processes**

3. **Compare the process capability to best practices, benchmarks, and competitors' capabilities**

4. **Assess historical performance/capability and the implications environmental demands have on the process architecture**

5. **Identify strengths/weaknesses**

6. **Begin preliminary analysis**

Sample questions:

- Which processes are most strategic?
- What is the capability of your most strategic processes?

TOOLS

In addition to the Value Chain Analysis discussed in Activity 2.1, the following tool will also be helpful.

PHASE 2, TOOL 2: PROCESS HIERARCHY TEMPLATE

A thorough understanding of how work gets done in your organization is just as important as any external input in terms of mapping a road to success. In addition to reviewing the technology and organization components noted above, leaders should make time to review the internal processes for insights into both competitive advantage and organizational weaknesses.

The process hierarchy tool can be used to catalog the processes within an organization. It can be used to visualize processes and can help you understand how processes interface with the structure. In addition to the steps noted above, leaders should ensure all process documentation is reviewed (noting what is missing and/or incomplete).

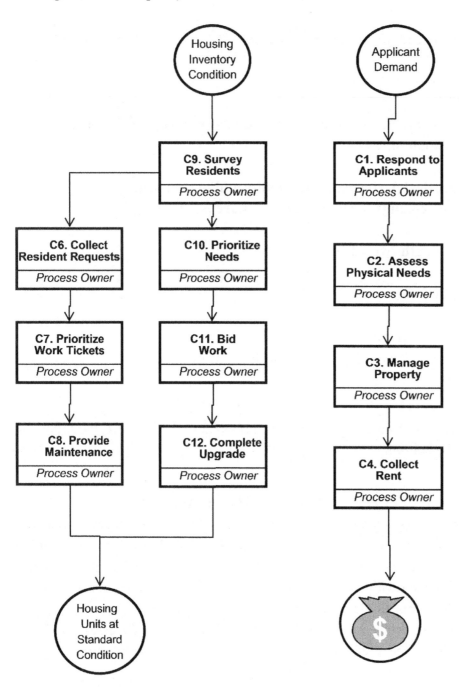

This tool can be used to facilitate discussions around the likely impacts any design changes will have on each element of architecture.

Make sure you spend sufficient time vetting each element of architecture. This matrix can be used to ensure your future-state design solution for your organization addresses all the necessary change management elements.

DELIVERABLE

Completing this step will provide the following for use in your overall strategic plan:

C. Process Architecture Summary

ACTIVITY 2.4: COMPLETE FINANCIAL AND OPERATIONAL ANALYSIS

WHAT IS IT?

This activity has two components.

1. Financial Analysis. This involves conducting a historical review of the financial performance of your organization. It typically focuses on such things as a trend analysis of revenues, profitability, cash flow, and debt levels. Once completed it is important to collect as much similar information as possible on your competitor's financial performance to understand how their performance compares to yours. This will also provide useful intelligence on a competitor's future actions based on their financial limitations.

2. Operational Analysis. This builds on some of your earlier work. The focus here is on fully understanding how you deliver your core product/service to identify strengths, weaknesses, or sources of competitive advantage. For example, if a competitor's cost to deliver a service is 20% lower than yours, it's important to understand the reasons behind that. What can you do differently?

TASKS

Completing the following will help ensure you secure the greatest benefit from your financial and operational analysis.

1. Identify the key financial performance criteria to review

Collect data and complete a three-year trend analysis on such variables as:

- Revenues/profitability
- Return on assets
- Cost of goods sold (COGS)
- Earnings per share (EPS)
- Debt/equity ratio
- Profitability by product, market, customer, and channel

2. Compare and contrast your financial results with the industry leader and other competitors over the same time horizon

- What lessons can be extrapolated?
- What can you do differently?

3. Begin preliminary analysis

Compare the following elements:

- Sales/profitability by competitor
- Cash flow
- Short- and long-term borrowing capability (debt/equity ratio)
- Sales/working capital ratio year to year
- Sales/materials ratio by competitor
- Administrative costs
- Facilities costs

4. Compare operational capabilities

- Customer satisfaction/brand loyalty (comparison to competitors)
- Product mix/breadth
- Product quality
- Relative cost

- New product introductions
- Core capabilities
- Channel coverage/quality
- Strength of channel relationships
- Marketing and sales (market research, sales force)
- Operations (manufacturing cost, learning curve, economies of scale, skill, locations of assets, degree of integration, flexibility of operations)
- R&D

TOOLS

To ensure you conduct the most comprehensive financial and operational analysis we recommend the use of the following tool. Please note that this tool focuses primarily on the financial component, which is more easily standardized across industries. The operational element often requires customization to reflect the needs/realities of a specific organization.

PHASE 2, TOOL 3: HISTORICAL FINANCIAL ANALYSIS TEMPLATE

This tool should be customized to your unique needs. It allows you to capture key financial performance and operational capabilities data by product/service for your organization. We recognize that historical performance is important; however, given the pace of business, it's helpful to focus on a medium-term perspective – e.g., a three-year window.

Products	**Year 1**	**Year 2**	**Year 3**
I. Financial Performance			
Total revenues			
Total debt			
Current ratio			

Products	Year 1	Year 2	Year 3
Asset turnover			
II. Operational Performance			
Cycle time of key processes			
Flexibility			
Responsiveness			
III. Customer/Market Performance			
Product A revenues			
Product B revenues			
Product C revenues			
Key customer retention			
Customer satisfaction			

DELIVERABLE

Completing this step will provide the following for use in your overall strategic plan:

D. Financial Analysis Summary

ACTIVITY 2.5: IDENTIFY STRENGTHS

WHAT IS IT?

During the first three activities in this phase the organization's technology, organization, and process architecture were analyzed. This provides the source data to complete activities 2.5 and 2.6. Additionally, it can be used to assess how well the core capabilities and competencies align with the needs of the markets served by the organization. Examples of strengths include:

- Strong executive leadership
- Strong brand equity
- Low-cost manufacturer

Core capabilities are defined as the general functional or content strengths of an organization. This is often communicated from the context that a certain company is acknowledged as being excellent at a particular competency. For example, Procter & Gamble is known as a marketing organization, while 3M is perceived to be exceptional at new product development.

Competencies are defined as the knowledge, skills, and abilities resident in the employee population. Different strategic alternatives require different core capabilities and competencies.

A competency assessment is used to identify the gaps between the existing competencies and those the workforce needs to achieve the new business strategy. This activity needs to be tightly aligned with the human capital or workforce planning processes enterprise-wide. You may need to acquire new talent to be able to capture a potential target market.

TASKS

Completing the following will help you develop a complete picture of your organization's strengths.

1. **Review available data. Sources include:**
   - Historical management reports
   - Feedback from customers

- Aggregate talent management/succession planning summary
- Human capital plan
- Benchmarks/best practices
- Feedback from employees, suppliers, channel partners

2. Identify capabilities and competencies needed to meet the requirements of the market

- What parts of the value chain are most strategic?
- Which items, though important would not yield additional competitive advantage if investments / focus on the area was enhanced? Remember, having a firm grasp on the tactical / delivery oriented elements will help highlight that which is truly strategic.

3. Identify core competencies by major unit or job family

- Industry expertise
- Product/service expertise
- Technical/technology
- Leadership
- Functional

4. Identify architecture, core capability, and competency strengths

TOOLS

The following tools will help you develop an accurate picture of your organization's strategic strengths.

PHASE 2, TOOL 4: PRODUCT / SERVICE ATTRIBUTES VS. INTERNAL CAPABILITIES WORKSHEET

This tool enables you to look at individual products/services both in terms of their specific attributes and in terms of your organization's current capabilities in areas that directly affect those offerings. This unique view will help you identify areas within your organization that can be leveraged in pursuit of turning out the best possible offering as well as those departments that need to be up-skilled/overhauled if they are to make a positive impact in service to the customer.

Product / Service Attributes	Purchasing	Sales	Marketing	R&D	Distribution	Logistics	Ops	IT
Price								
Product features								
Service								
Quality								
Delivery								

PHASE 2, TOOL 5: CAPABILITIES VS. IMPORTANCE MATRIX

Compiling this information will allow you to complete the next tool – the capabilities/importance matrix. This will provide a visual depiction of where your organization should devote its collective energy.

Please note: This data is designed to provide an accurate representation of the current state. Business leaders should consider the future direction and speed of change for their industry and overlay that reality on this "as-is" assessment. This is critical, and will help ensure you don't win at a sport no longer played or fail to enter a game that's just being invented.

Capabilities vs. Importance Matrix
Phase 2, Tool 5

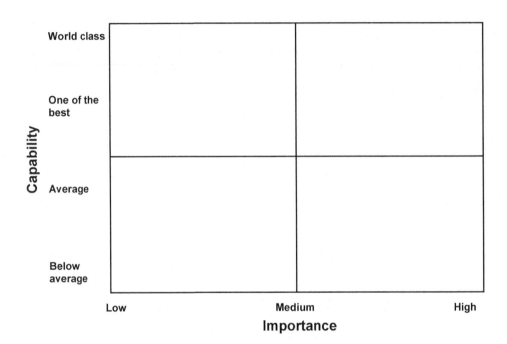

PHASE 2, TOOL 6: COMPETITIVE ASSESSMENT TABLE

The final tool in this section will help you compare your organization with your most important/influential competitors using a series of critical factors. Sample factors are listed in the chart below, but others can be added to better reflect your industry.

Variable	Company	Competitor 1	Competitor 2	Competitor 3
Product quality				
Service quality				
Price				
Manufacturing cost				
Breadth of product line				
Sales force				
New product development				

DELIVERABLES

Completing this step will provide the following for use in your overall strategic plan:

E. Summary of Strengths

ACTIVITY 2.6: IDENTIFY WEAKNESSES

WHAT IS IT?

Most organizations do not spend enough time identifying their weaknesses. It is important to identify these to be able to better understand your probability of success relative to strategic alternatives. It also helps to clarify what actions (addressing performance/capability gaps) need to be undertaken to ensure strategy execution.

Examples of weaknesses include:

- High-cost, slow-response supply chain
- Weak sales-prospecting process
- R&D has poor track record in bringing new products to market

TASKS

Completing the following will help ensure you develop a complete picture of your organization's weaknesses.

1. Review all data collected during this phase of work
- Historical management reports
- Feedback from customers
- Benchmarks/best practices
- Feedback from employees, suppliers, channel partners

2. Identify performance gaps
- Customer satisfaction
- Rate or referral / repeat customers

3. Identify capabilities and competences needed to meet the requirements of the market

4. Confirm core competencies by major function or job family such as:
- Industry expertise
- Product/service expertise
- Technical/technology
- Leadership
- Functional

5. Prioritize architecture, core capability, and competency weaknesses

TOOLS

The tools listed in Activity 2.5 should also be used in this stage of the analysis.

DELIVERABLE

Completing this step will provide the following for use in your strategic plan.

F. Summary of Weaknesses

ACTIVITY 2.7: IDENTIFY SOURCE OF COMPETITIVE ADVANTAGE

WHAT IS IT?

An organizational strength is not necessarily a source of competitive advantage. Strengths may not map directly to such things as customers' unmet needs or desired purchasing criteria. The two must align for there to be a source of competitive advantage.

TASKS

Completing the following will help ensure you look beyond the basics and develop a realistic picture of your areas of competitive advantage.

1. **Review appropriate customer/market data**
    - Desired product/service attributes
    - Unmet needs
    - Sources of dissatisfaction

2. **Compare your capabilities to those of your competitors**
    Be sure to focus on elements referenced in sections 2.1 and 2.2 of this document – your technology and organizational architecture.

3. **Identify a short list of variables that are your true sources of competitive advantage**

TOOLS

The Competitive Assessment table referenced in Activity 2.5 can also be helpful at this stage of the analysis.

DELIVERABLE

G. **Sources of Competitive Advantage**

PHASE 3: STRATEGY DEVELOPMENT

PURPOSE

This phase is by far the most important in the process. It involves analyzing the data collected during the prior research-oriented phases and evaluating a variety of alternative strategies against a number of objective decision filters to ensure the best possible strategy is selected. This effort will then be translated into a comprehensive balanced scorecard of metrics that are cascaded throughout the organization. **Figure 5** below illustrates the various activities required for developing the organization's strategy.

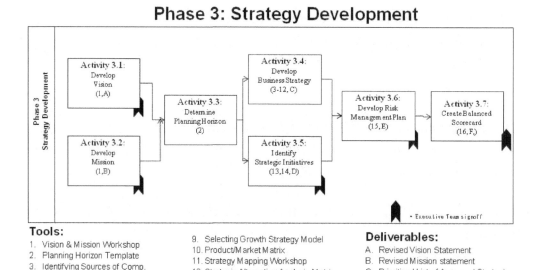

Figure 5: Strategic Planning Phase 3 – Strategy Development

While all internal and external inputs are helpful, it's critical when completing this portion of the work that you have tightly aligned your HR practices – such as rewards/recognition, talent acquisition, performance management, human capital planning, and leadership development – to your strategy.

People are often the drivers of success, especially in service-oriented organizations. To be effective, they have to understand, support, and feel able and motivated to execute the strategy. This will be covered more fully in Phase 4 – Strategy Deployment, but it is helpful to keep the end game in mind during the design phase. Build something that sparks cultural organ rejection and you may find yourself in jeopardy.

TOOLS AND DELIVERABLES

Figure 5 above references the expected deliverables from Phase 3 as well as the tools that enable their development. The key deliverables during this part of the strategic planning process are an approved strategy, a list of strategic initiatives, a risk management plan, an enterprise-wide scorecard that holds people accountable, and a robust communication plan to ensure all employees and stakeholders understand the way forward and their role in making it happen.

Leaders often get sidetracked at this stage. The desire to "boil the ocean" can be tempting. However, it's important to stick to those actions that will yield the greatest ROI. To ensure you get the most from your efforts, keep the following guidelines in mind.

- Stay away from "feel-good" work. Unless your organization is at the proverbial crossroads, don't spend a lot of time developing a vision and mission statement – the reality is nobody cares!
- Developing a business strategy is much more than simply identifying the strategic initiatives your organization will undertake. It's all about specificity – identifying specifically what markets you enter or exit. It's about how much revenue you expect to generate from each internal and external growth engine. And it's about the big-picture questions you must answer to obtain the proverbial "win."
- Develop a plan for evolving the culture to closely support your business plan. Create consequences for desired and undesired values, behaviors, and results.

WHO IS ACCOUNTABLE?

Unlike the other phases, where data is gathered with the intention of using these insights to drive opinions and insights, Phase 3 is a time for leaders to lead. Having received and considered all the input from various internal and external parties, the senior leadership team must make the call. The leader, be it the CEO, GM, or actual business owner, must take ultimate ownership of and accountability for these decisions. It is not something that can be delegated to the vice president of strategy planning.

While this might seem like a no-brainer, too often senior leadership abrogates their responsibility and relies on excessive consensus decision-making instead of making the tough decisions. To be credible and effective, the upper echelon of an organization must visibly own the strategic plan. Overlooking this responsibility is the primary reason strategic plans go unnoticed.

ACTIVITY 3.1: DEVELOP OR UPDATE VISION (SITUATIONAL)

WHAT IS IT?

A vision is a description of the future state of the organization five or more years into the future. It should be used to create images for employees on where the organization is going and engage their hearts and minds to help you get there.

Our experience suggests that, in many cases, far too much time is spent on activities 3.1 and 3.2 – designing touchy-feely vision and mission statements. This is a byproduct of senior executives lacking strong strategic thinking skills and not understanding where to invest time in the strategic planning process. We are unaware of any organization realizing competitive advantage by having the best-written vision or mission statement. Enron had a mission statement, and so did many now-defunct financial institutions.

TASKS

When needed, completing the following will help you develop the vision statement:

1. **Determine who will be involved in the vision development**

This can be a cross section of employees, the senior management team, or a combination. The selection is usually based on the organization's culture and how dramatic the shift from the current state will be. While it is helpful to engage employees to build buy-in, sometimes they lack the big-picture view to conceptualize and articulate the future state of the organization.

Note: In those cases where top leaders craft the vision in isolation, it's important to shop/socialize the new vision in a cascading fashion to ensure you build understanding and support across the organization.

2. **Facilitate a visioning workshop**

To use all attendees' time most efficiently we suggest you develop a pre-work assignment so that participants come to the workshop ready to participate. Evaluate the vision drafts using the following questions:

- Is it future focused? (5–10 years planning horizon)
- Will it help guide stakeholder actions?
- Is it brief and clear?
- Does it engender passion and commitment?
- Does it provide an ideal desired end state?
- Does it offer guiding principles and/or values?
- Does it communicate a "burning platform" or business case?

3. **Evolve the vision statement**

Obtain appropriate feedback to improve the vision statement. Listed below are several evaluation questions:

- Does the vision move people to action?
- Is it easy to understand?
- Is it a "stretch" from the current state, yet still believable?
- Is it linked to the needs of customers or the market?
- Can you determine ways to execute the vision through business and function-specific strategies?

TOOLS

To help develop the best possible vision, use the following tool:

PHASE 3, TOOL 1: VISION AND MISSION WORKSHOP

Most seasoned leaders have sat through the writing exercise known as visioning. All too often you have a number of highly compensated leaders debating whether to use the word "a" or "the." Our experience suggests that this exercise is only useful when a company is at a fundamental crossroads and either pathway will be distinctly different from the status quo.

Below are some guidelines that can be used to facilitate a fast-cycle workshop focused on developing a workable draft of both a vision and mission. Once completed, craft an offline assignment to develop more refined working drafts. This will save a considerable amount of senior management time and shorten the overall cycle time.

Guideline 1: Provide a brief definition of the terms to ensure all stakeholders have the same point of reference.

Vision Statement:
- Future focused (5–10 years planning horizon)
- Typically addresses the following elements:
  - Desired end state
  - Guiding principles and/or values

Mission Statement:
- Focused on the present
- Typically addresses the following elements:
  - Purpose
  - How you add value (i.e., product or services delivered)
  - Customers/markets served

Guideline 2: Review characteristics of well-written vision and mission statements.

A Well-Written Vision Statement:
- Is future focused
- Is used to guide actions in the immediate term

- Is clear and concise
- Engenders passion and commitment
- Is a "guiding star"
- Is updated at key milestones
- Is perceived as a "burning platform" or business case

A Well-Written Mission Statement:
- Is grounded in what you are doing today
- Communicates a clear statement of the reason you exist
- Drives to specificity

Guideline 3: Review samples of well-written vision and mission statements.

Vision statement samples:
- **GE** – Become number one or number two in every market we serve and revolutionize this company to have the strengths of a big company combined with the leanness and agility of a small company.
- **NASA** – To understand and protect our home planet; to explore the Universe and search for life; to inspire the next generation of explorers … as only NASA can.
- **Bayer Diagnostics**
  o We will earn the loyalty of our Customers by being the people that Customers want to do business with because we relentlessly strive to exceed their expectations. We will create an irresistible force that attracts and sustains customer loyalty.
  o We consistently will be among the leading, fastest growing diagnostics companies by rapidly creating and delivering innovative healthcare solutions.
  o Quality is in our hearts, minds, and spirits. It encompasses all of our activities at all times. By our actions, we are living examples of how to communicate, measure, recognize, reward, and continuously improve quality.
  o Together we will build an organization that inspires personal, professional, and business success.

Mission statement samples:
- **Global Consulting Company** - We provide M&A advisory services including due diligence and post acquisition integration to small (from $50MM to $200MM) and mid-cap companies (from $500MM to $1BB) in the Financial Services, Banking, and Private Equity industries located in North America and Europe. Our services enhance shareholder value, shorten the cycle time of deals, and increase the capture of targeted synergies.
  - Note that it highlights services delivered, markets/customers, and value added
- **BHBU** – We develop and commercialize products and services that bring value to the Behavioral Health community around the world.
- **Bayer Diagnostics** – Bayer Diagnostics will make a positive difference to human health … daily

Guideline 4: Establish guidelines for tone and structure personalized to the organization's culture.

As you can see from the samples in Guideline 3, when done correctly the vision and mission statements of different companies should sound *different*. Leaders should avoid "no-brainer" or politically correct language as it often fails to add value or inspire employees.

NASA's vision inspires because it uses long-term, explorer-oriented language that speaks to the adventurer in us all. Bayer's mission, while lacking the traditional specificity endorsed above, passionately conveys the reason employees come to work each day.

Note: Many organizations take this time to review their **corporate values** or guiding principles. This can be a powerful additive when aligned to the vision and overarching corporate culture. The following is an example from an aerospace and defense organization.

- **Vision** – We are in the business of supplying aerospace components and related high tech products. In running our business, we are dedicated to fulfilling our responsibility to our company's stockholders, our customers, our employees, our owners, our communities, and our suppliers.

- **Guiding Principles and Values:**
  - Put the customer first
  - Conduct our business using the highest standard of ethics and corporate citizenship
  - Lead by example using the principles and values
  - Utilize TQM principles
  - Be uncompromising in our standards
  - Maintain a respect for the individual
  - Empower people to make decisions in the best interest of our customers and our company
  - Reward people consistent with individual, team, and organizational performance
  - Operate our business to protect the well-being of our employees

Guideline 5: Craft the first draft of your Vision and Mission Statements.

The following instructions will help your team create a draft vision statement:

1. Review prior vision statements, current business plans, and other relevant input.
2. Imagine a picture of the future of your company that describes what it is like to work in this new environment.
3. You will be provided 3x5 Post-it notes to use to identify key words that describe the desired end state of the company 5–10 years in the future. Post them at the front of the room.
4. You will be provided with five "dots" to vote on the key words you feel have the most merit (one vote per key word).
5. You will be provided with additional Post-its to identify the "values" or "guiding principles" needed to achieve the desired end state (use value cards). Post them in the front of the room.
6. You will be provided with five "dots" to vote on the "guiding principles and/or values" you feel have the most merit (one vote per "principle").
7. Using the key values that received the highest votes, break into your groups and brainstorm behaviors that reflect each value.
8. You will be provided with five "dots" to vote on the "behaviors that support each key value" (one vote per "behavior").

The following steps will help you create a draft mission statement.

1. Review the company vision, any modifications to the earlier vision, and the current business plan as primary inputs.
2. You will be provided with 3x5 Post-its to use to identify key words that describe the "Purpose" of the organization. Post them at the front of the room.
3. You will be provided with five "dots" to vote on the "key words" you feel have the most merit (one vote per "key word").
4. You will be provided with additional Post-its to identify the "products/services/value added" and "customer/markets served" needed to achieve vision. Post them at the front of the room.
5. You will be provided with five "dots" to vote on the items in step 4 you feel have the most merit (one vote per item).
6. We will now break you into vision and mission sub-teams. Each sub-team will be tasked with assembling all the "key words" into a cogent vision and mission statement, which they will present to the entire group, noting any additional revisions.

Guideline 6: Review a series of test questions that will help evaluate your efforts thus far – this avoids committing to an untested path.

Vision Test Questions:
1. Does the vision move people to action?
2. Is it easy to understand?
3. Is it a "stretch" from the current state, yet still believable?
4. Is it linked to customers' needs?
5. Can you determine ways to execute the vision through business and function-specific strategies?

Mission Test Questions:
1. Does the mission cascade from your business plan and vision statement?
2. Is it clear enough that a layperson would understand what you do?
3. Does it clearly articulate your purpose, what customers or markets you serve, and how you add value?

Once you have the draft vision and mission statements, it's important to consider the next steps before commencing with the rollout process. The following questions will help frame your action plan:

- When completed, how do you intend to use the vision and mission statement?
- Will you solicit any additional stakeholders for their input? If so, who and how?
- How will you communicate the vision and mission statements?
- Are there any modifications you need to make to your short-term or medium-term business plan to better align it to your updated vision and mission?
- Are there any other rollout issues you need to address?
- What are the next steps, roles, and timelines?

DELIVERABLE

Completing this step will provide the following for use in your overall strategic plan.

A. Revised Vision Statement

ACTIVITY 3.2: DEVELOP OR UPDATE MISSION (SITUATIONAL)

WHAT IS IT?

A well-written mission statement is grounded in what you are doing today and communicates a clear statement of the reason you exist. Mission statements typically:

- Are focused on the present
- Articulate the organization's purpose
- Demonstrate how you add value (i.e., product or services delivered)
- Highlight the customers/markets served

TASKS

Completing the following will help ensure you design the best possible mission statement:

1. Facilitate a mission statement workshop (this can be done separately or concurrently with the vision statement)

To use all attendees' time most efficiently we suggest you develop a pre-work assignment so that participants come to the workshop prepared. Evaluate the drafts using the following questions:

- How do you intend to use the mission statement?
- Is it clear enough that a layperson would understand what you do?
- Does it clearly articulate your purpose, what customers or markets you serve, and how you add value?

2. Share with a broader audience to obtain their input and pre-sell the final deliverable

TOOL

The Vision and Mission Workshop listed in Activity 3.1 is also used to complete this activity.

DELIVERABLE

Completing this step will provide the following for use in your strategic plan.

B. Revised Mission Statement

ACTIVITY 3.3: DETERMINE PLANNING HORIZON

WHAT IS IT?

Planning horizon refers to how many years in the future the strategic plan covers. This can range from two years to twenty.

Organizations often default to whatever time horizon they have used in the past, as opposed to selecting a planning horizon that is appropriate for their market conditions. A planning horizon that is too short turns your strategic planning process into a to-do list and one that is too long in a volatile environment turns your process into a creative writing event.

TASKS

Completing the following will help ensure you select the most appropriate planning horizon.

1. Assess the key decision variables to determine the planning horizon

Examples include:

- Volatility of the market
- Predictability of the market
- Length of product/service lifecycles
- Size of the organization
- Rate of technical innovation
- Capital intensity of the industry

2. Identify the relationships between each decision variable and the planning horizon

For each of the decision variables noted in Task 1 above there is a positive correlation. For example, the more predictable the market, the longer the planning horizon you can tolerate.

3. **Determine the final planning horizon**
    Before finalizing your horizon, assess the planning horizon of your current competitors. Compare yours to theirs for reasonableness. Make changes as needed.

TOOLS
To identify your planning horizon use the following tool.

PHASE 3, TOOL 2: PLANNING HORIZON TEMPLATE
This tool is used to determine how many years your strategic plan will cover. In some instances (e.g., you are part of a conglomerate) this will be mandated by corporate.

For each criterion place an "x" along the continuum that most closely approximates your organization. The planning horizon is determined by aggregating where most of the criteria fall. For example, if most of the criteria fall halfway between five and ten years, then the planning horizon is probably seven to eight years long.

Completed Planning Horizon Template

Planning Horizon Variables	Planning Continuum	
Volatility of market	High	Low
Level of competition	Intense	Relaxed
Predictability of market	Low	High
Length of product lifecycle	Short	Long
Growth of market	Fast	Slow
Rate of technical innovation	Fast	Slow
Capital intensity of industry	Low	High
Length of Planning Horizon	2–3 yrs 5 yrs >10yrs	

DELIVERABLE

While there are no specific deliverables for this task (beyond the selection of the planning horizon), the analysis will feed into other elements of the strategic plan.

ACTIVITY 3.4: DEVELOP BUSINESS STRATEGY

WHAT IS IT?

During this activity the data that was collected earlier is used to identify a number of strategic alternatives. The senior team should agree on several decision criteria to objectively evaluate each alternative.

Objective criteria are essential to ensure the strategies selected stand up to scrutiny and are not the outgrowth of strong personalities of key executives.

TASKS

Completing the following tasks is critical to developing a comprehensive business strategy.

1. Confirm your customers' desired purchase criteria, desired product/service attributes, and unmet needs

2. Identify market space/targeting

Market space/targeting is defined as organizing your markets into subgroups that have similar needs and/or decisions about the purchase/use of a given product or service. Markets are segmented by looking for groups of individuals with similar needs/characteristics who have similar purchase criteria. Markets can be segmented in a variety of ways. Below are two different approaches:

- Consumer markets
    - Geographic
    - Demographic
    - Behavioral
- Business markets
    - Geographic

- o Behavioral
- o Attitudinal

Markets can also be segmented according to customer needs. To do this, take the time to identify unmet customer needs and segment accordingly.

Once complete, obtain consensus on the **current** markets you will continue to compete in and identify **new** markets. Use the data collected below to guide your decision-making:

- Market size
- Market profitability
- Market growth rates
- Current market share
- Current revenues
- Competitors' strength
- Barriers to entry/exit

3. **Finalize positioning**

Consider the following questions as you finalize your analysis:

- What is the competition doing?
- Where do you have an advantage over your competitors?
- What is your positioning statement? You can focus on:
  - o Product feature
  - o Feature performance
  - o Unmet need
  - o Price value
  - o User group

Once complete, develop a formal positioning statement for *each* customer segment. Consider the following questions:

- Who are the target customers?
- What is the offering that links directly to met/unmet customer needs?
- What current markets will you continue in?
- What new products/markets will you enter?
- What is the benefit?

4. Determine strategy/value proposition

Strategy answers the question "What do you plan to do?" The business strategy is an integrated set of actions that is directed at achieving sustainable (not easily copied) competitive advantage. Address the following:

- Rationalize the product and business portfolio
- What are the final offerings (products/service by market segment)?
- Determine the business model needed to implement each strategic alternative (how does each element of your architecture – technology, organization, process – need to be configured?)
- What organizational capabilities are needed to deploy each strategic alternative

For each strategy, note the underlying assumptions and risks. For example, "Over the next five years governmental spending for health care will increase by 12% per year" is an assumption that needs to be accounted for.

5. Identify internal capability gaps

To help with this process, consider the following:

- To what degree do your current capabilities allow you to realistically capture market opportunities?
- What specific gaps do you have regarding the current capabilities of your technology, organization, and process architectures?
- What specific resources will you need to build additional capability?

6. Develop Market Strategy

Review e-scan data, particularly regarding unmet needs, customer buyer criteria, and sources/causes of dissatisfaction. Then determine the 4 P's: product, place, promotion, and price, according to the following guidelines.

- **Product** strategies relate to the features of the item in question.
  - O Features/functions
  - O Service/warranty
  - O Options
- **Place** strategies relate to where products are manufactured and sold. Examples include:
  - O Distribution channels

O Asset location

O Inventory volumes

- **Promotion** strategies relate to how the product is communicated to create awareness in the market. This includes such things as:
  - O Advertising (target audiences, media used, budget)
  - O Promotion (rebates, discounts, etc.)
  - O Public relations
- **Pricing** strategies are the engine for customer acquisition. Variables to address include:
  - O Use and terms around discounting
  - O Returns and allowances
  - O Payment period
  - O Credit terms

TOOLS

As this is the most involved stage of the process, a variety of tools is needed to ensure the development of a robust business strategy. To that end, use the following:

PHASE 3, TOOL 3: IDENTIFYING SOURCES OF COMPETITIVE ADVANTAGE

An organization's strength does not always correlate to a source of competitive advantage. Asking stakeholders often results in answers based largely on bravado rather than reality.

Most organizations truly don't know the difference between a strength and a source of competitive advantage. In column one, identify all of your organization's core capabilities. In the subsequent columns, identify competitiveness variables. In some instances, you might want to weight the variables in terms of importance. Develop a schema (high, medium, low; or quantitative numbers) to evaluate the importance of each core capability. The core capabilities that get the highest score are an indicator of your sources of competitive advantage.

Core Capabilities	Decision Variables				
	Performance relative to competition	Directly drive top- or bottom-line financial performance	Key to meeting customer requirements	Option 4	Option 5
Access to raw materials	M	M	L		
Proprietary technology	H	M	L		
Product offering	H	H	H		
Distribution network	M	H	H		

This tool can be customized in a variety of ways. You might want to start with the core capabilities of your firm. These capabilities can then be rated relative to market dynamics, customer requirements, comparison to competitors' capabilities, etc. By selecting the right criteria and incorporating a vetting process, stakeholders can be engaged to reach consensus around the true sources of competitive advantage

PHASE 3, TOOL 4: MARKET ATTRACTIVENESS/BUSINESS SEGMENT MATRIX

This tool can be used in conjunction with the previous tools to refine where you want to compete.

Columns two and three are used to **score** and **weight** each of the **market attractiveness** and **ability to compete variables**. The analysis can be further defined by breaking down markets into smaller business segments.

Customer Data	Score	Weighting	Segment/ Business 1	Segment / Business 2	Segment / Business 3	Segment / Business 4
I. Market Attractiveness						
Competitive Intensity						
Barriers to entry/exit						
Buyer power						
Profitability						
Market size						
#/strength of competitors						
Threat of disruptive technology						
Threat from substitute products						
II. Ability to Compete						
Market share						
Fit with core capabilities						
Offerings vs. unmet needs						

Customer Data	Score	Weighting	Segment/ Business 1	Segment / Business 2	Segment / Business 3	Segment / Business 4
Access to suppliers/ channel partners/ distributers						
Possess resources to meet market needs						

PHASE 3, TOOL 5: ADJACENT MARKET OPPORTUNITY TEMPLATE

Adjacency is a growth strategy that focuses on expansion from the core business/core competency into related segments or businesses that draw from the strength of the core business. This type of growth strategy leverages existing customer relationships, technology, intellectual capital, and core competencies to accelerate the growth into the adjacent market.

This tool can be used to identify adjacent growth options, evaluate each option, and select the best strategy.

1. Identify potential adjacency growth options. Collect appropriate and available data on such variables as different market segments, customer feedback, unmet customer needs, benchmarks, etc. This data can be sourced from trade groups, professional associations, and data aggregators, as well as from your sales force, marketing function, suppliers, and channel partners.

Use this data to identify all of the potential adjacent markets. This can be visualized by using a bubble map – see sample on next page.

Tips:
- Do not evaluate the alternatives prematurely. As with brainstorming, the initial focus must be on identifying all of the potential adjacent markets.
- Rather than generating alternatives in a haphazard manner, use the data to inform your thinking.

Bubble Diagram to Visualize Adjacent Markets

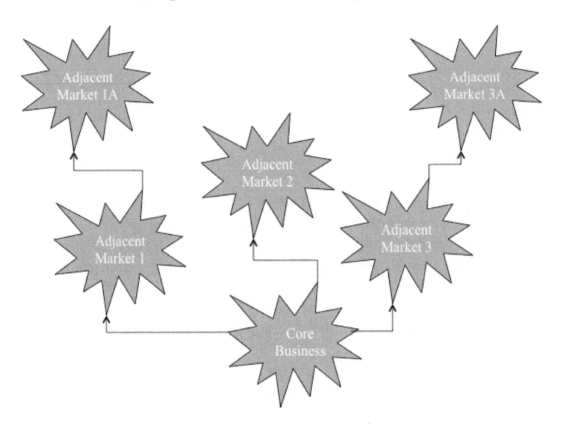

2. Evaluate each adjacency growth option. Obtain consensus around the specific decision filters you will use to prioritize the adjacent growth options. This data can be collected via a number of tools, such as market forecasts, competitive landscape analysis, and scenario analysis. Examples include:

- Unmet customer/market needs
- Market growth rate
- Competitors
- Fit with business strategy/value proposition
- Market profitability
- Market size

Tips:

- Once you have consensus around the decision criteria, create a matrix and use **quantitative** (high, medium, low) means to evaluate each growth option. This will reduce the effect of strong personalities and individual agendas adversely impacting the process.
- Not all decision criteria are equally important. You might find it useful to weight each criterion.

3. Make sure you can realize "finalist" growth options. History is littered with train wrecks of companies that went after a potential market but were unable to capture what was theoretically there. The two most common reasons for failure are insufficient resources (budget, headcount, etc.) and poor fit with the organization's core capabilities. The latter is particularly challenging. Make sure that for the finalist adjacent market opportunities you ask the tough questions:

- What are the core capabilities needed to be successful in the adjacent market?
- Are there sub-markets that require different core capabilities?
- Are there any capability gaps? If so, how can these gaps be addressed?

PHASE 3, TOOL 6: NEW PRODUCT EVALUATION TEMPLATE

Growth can be achieved through external (e.g., M&A, JVs, licensing, partnerships) and internal (e.g., the 4 P's, new product introduction) growth engines.

This tool will help consider factors associated with the internal growth engine. Specifically, this tool can be used to:

- Define a new product idea
- Identify the risks/underlying assumptions
- Objectively evaluate each concept
- Select the best new product-development opportunity

To make the best use of this resource, complete the following steps:

1. Confirm Strategic Alignment and Market Attractiveness. Listed below are some questions you should answer:

Strategic Alignment Questions:
- How does the proposed new product align with your business plan?
- What is the primary strategic reason for considering this new product? Is it to protect/sustain the current business, fill a gap in the product line, match a competitor, beat a competitor in the market, enter a new market segment, enter a new geographic market, or gain access to a technology?
- What will happen if you do not develop the proposed new product?
- How does the new product fit with the other strategic priorities in your business?
- What is your source of competitive advantage? What is the patent position of the proposed solution? What trade secrets does your organization possess?
- Do you have a cost advantage?

Market Alignment Questions:
- What unmet need does it address in the market?
- Does the customer recognize the need for this opportunity currently?
- How is it distinctly different? What are the benefits?
- What are the barriers to switching?
- Who is the buyer?
- How is the market segment defined? What are the major sub-segments? In which market sub-segment does this opportunity fit?
- What is the size of the market in units and dollars?
- What is the growth rate at an aggregate level and by segment? What is driving or restraining growth? Are some sub-segments of the market growing faster than others?
- What regions/countries should be targeted initially? Why?
- What regions/countries have long-term potential? Why?
- What regions/countries will not be targeted? Why?
- What are the major differences in customer requirements by region/country?

Competition Questions:
- Who is the competition? What are their sources of competitive advantage?
- What are the substitute products?
- Are there any disruptive technologies that are a risk?
- What is the current market share for the competition? How has market share changed over the last three years?
- Overall, how competitive is this market?

Competency Alignment Questions:
- Do we have needed capabilities (e.g., marketing infrastructure, manufacturing expertise) to develop and manufacture this product?
- What are the needed operations, technical skills, and sales and marketing competency requirements?
- What are the key gaps? How can they be ameliorated (education, hiring, strategic partnership)?

Tips:
- Identify, collect, and use data to drive your decision-making. Avoid "I think," "I feel" discussions.
- Remember that alignment with the business plan and enterprise-wide scorecard along with market opportunities drive the decision. Avoid pet projects and do not succumb to strong personalities. Data must drive your go/no-go decision.

2. Obtain Consensus on the Financial Projections. Questions to answer include:
- What are the underlying assumptions behind the projections?
- How will segment share (advertising, education, PR, etc.) for the proposed solution grow over time?
- Will you take share from existing competitors?
- How will the price point evolve over time? How will that impact market share?
- How does the timing of market entry impact the projected market share? What if you entered later (or sooner)?
- Will this proposed product cannibalize any of your current products?

Which ones? How much?

- Will this proposed product increase sales of your other products? Which ones? How much?
- Will you be able to leverage current resources (sales force, professional education)?
- What are the bottom-line financials? How does the project compare with the business's hurdle rates?
- When will you launch this opportunity?
- What are the year five sales? What is the year five gross profit percentage?
- What is the Net Present Value (NPV)?
- What is the estimated investment from today through launch?
- Does the project fail to meet any existing hurdle rates? Which ones?

Tips:

- Utilize your financial business partners or outside accounting firm to provide the necessary expertise.
- Develop a detailed P&L and NPV analysis, with a breakdown of revenues (including how unit sales were calculated) and costs for all targeted regions/countries.
- Fully document all assumptions and risks.

3. If Approved, How Will the Product Be Commercialized? Answer the following questions:

Compliance Plan

- Are the compliance, quality, and regulatory issues for each of the targeted regions/countries adequately addressed?
- What is the estimated total cost of the compliance plan?
- How long will it take? When would it begin?
- What are the major activities?

Operations Plan

- How will the new product be manufactured?
- Can manufacturing be done using existing facilities and equipment?

- Will third-party manufacturers be used? If yes, which ones?
- What is the sourcing plan?
- What are proposed packaging requirements?
- What are the environmental considerations?
- What incremental activities are required to address any regional differences?
- What is the targeted cost of goods sold?
- What are the major components of the targeted COGS?

Marketing Plan
- What is the go-to-market strategy?
- What are the major promotional activities and expenses?
- Can the existing sales force be used to sell the product?
- What is the estimated sales expense? Why?
- What is the estimated distribution expense? Why?
- What is the best channel in which to introduce this product?
- What is the strategy for distribution in the targeted regions/countries?
- Will customer education be needed? How much?
- What sales training will be needed?
- What are the major marketing research activities and expenses?
- What incremental activities are required to address any regional differences?

Miscellaneous:
- What are the product labeling and literature requirements?
- What is the strategy for trademark clearance?
- What will the internal pricing be for affiliate countries?

Risk:
- What are the risks that have the highest probability of occurrence with the greatest potential impact?
- Which of these risks can be minimized or eliminated? How?
- Is there a well-thought-out risk-mitigation plan?

4. Alternative Courses of Action. There are a myriad of growth options. What are the other growth strategies? Have you completed a financial, strategic-alignment, and risk assessment to ensure the proposed new product is the right option?

PHASE 3, TOOL 7: MARKET OPTIONS MATRIX

This tool can be used to better understand the current markets you compete in as well as identify potential future markets. Starting with column 2, the chart is constructed by identifying appropriate decision filters such as market size, growth rates, profitability, and rating and ranking current and potential markets.

Strategy identification is akin to going to a casino. It's not about having the best-written vision and mission; it's about placing your bets on your offering and the markets you will enter, exit, and compete in.

Market segments	Decision Variables							
	Size	Current Share	Growth Rate	Profitability	Barriers to Entry	Barrier to Exit	Competitive Intensity	Imp.
I. Current								
II. Potential								

PHASE 3, TOOL 8: PRODUCT / BUYER MATRIX – NOTED IN PHASE 1, TOOL 5

PHASE 3, TOOL 9: SELECTING GROWTH STRATEGY MODEL

The concept of growth is much harder to understand and implement than cost reduction. This four-box model will help you identify the most appropriate types of growth when you are considering:

- Current markets/current products
- New products/current markets
- Current products/new markets
- New products/new markets

Selecting a Growth Strategy Model

	Current Products	New Products
Current Markets	*Current products/ Current markets:* • 4P's (market strategy) • Advertising • Positioning	*New products/ Current markets:* • New product development • JV's • Alliances • Partnerships • Licensing • M&A • Backward/forward vertical integration
New Markets	*Current products/ New markets:* • 4P's (market strategy) • Alliances • Partnerships • New distribution channels (jobber, wholesaler, distributer)	*New product / New markets:* • 4P's (market strategy) • Alliances • Partnerships • New distribution channels (jobber, wholesaler,) • Backward/forward vertical integration

PHASE 3, TOOL 10: PRODUCT / MARKET MATRIX

The product market matrix can be configured using several variations. The sample below will help you review your offerings by market, performance, and internal capability.

Product/ Service	Market		Product Performance						Internal Capabilities	
	Size	Annual Growth Rate	Product Sales Volume	Product Profit Margins	Annual Product Sales Growth	Return on Sales	Return on Assets	Core Process	Talent
A										
B										
C										
D										

You can also refine the tool to review the following:

- Analyze current and potential offerings by market
- Compare and contrast your organization's offerings to those of current and potential competitors
- Evaluate your current offerings by customer set

PHASE 3, TOOL 11: STRATEGY MAPPING WORKSHOP

Originally developed by Robert Kaplan and David Norton, a strategy map is a complex tool that can be can be configured and used in a variety of ways.

In the example below the tool is configured to help identify the true "business drivers." Typically, you start with an overarching goal e.g., increasing return on capital employed (ROCE) and/or strategy (e.g., optimize customer satisfaction) and ask what drives those things. As you peel back the layers of the onion, you will find that the production process capability and logistics effectiveness are the business drivers you must focus on most.

How to Develop a Strategy Map

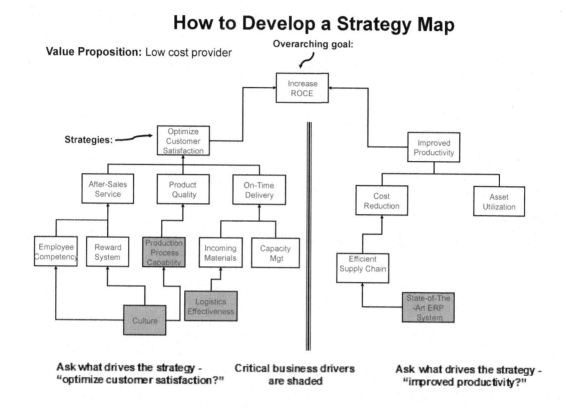

Value Proposition: Low cost provider

Overarching goal:

Increase ROCE

Strategies:

Optimize Customer Satisfaction

After-Sales Service

Product Quality

On-Time Delivery

Employee Competency

Reward System

Production Process Capability

Incoming Materials

Capacity Mgt

Culture

Logistics Effectiveness

Improved Productivity

Cost Reduction

Asset Utilization

Efficient Supply Chain

State-of-The-Art ERP System

Ask what drives the strategy - "optimize customer satisfaction?"

Critical business drivers are shaded

Ask what drives the strategy - "improved productivity?"

PHASE 3, TOOL 12: STRATEGIC ALTERNATIVE ANALYSIS MATRIX

Strategic planning is all about prioritization. Therefore, this tool is useful for prioritizing your short list of strategic alternatives based on objective criteria.

This tool can be completed by placing all of the shortlisted strategic alternatives in column one. The subsequent columns represent the specific decision filters you will use to prioritize the strategies. These are situational to each organization. It is often helpful to weight the decision filters since they are usually not equally important. For example: Low = 1, Medium = 3, High = 5.

Strategic Alternatives	Source of competitive advantage	Risk analysis	Degree of fit with culture	Degree of fit with capabilities	Budget available	Address opportunity & threats	Total
Strategy A							
Strategy B							
Strategy C							

DELIVERABLE

Completing this step will provide the following for use in your overall strategic plan.

C. Prioritized List of Approved Business Strategies

ACTIVITY 3.5: IDENTIFY STRATEGIC INITIATIVES

WHAT IS IT?

A common mistake made by organizations is to assume that a strategic plan is nothing more than a listing of strategic projects. However, it is much more than that.

Once the target markets, positioning, etc. have been agreed to, a number of strategic initiatives are commonly started in order to:

- Address major capability gaps
- Align the TOPS architecture to deploy the business plan; and/or
- Directly support one of the business strategies

TASKS

Completing the following will help you select the right strategies to execute.

1. Obtain consensus on the strategic initiatives

Identify a number of decision criteria and weight them if necessary. Use the criteria to objectively prioritize the initiatives. Make sure at least two of the criteria are some form of financial and risk analysis.

2. **Develop detailed charters for each approved initiative**
   A well-defined charter will address the following areas:
   - Core/ad hoc team members
   - Roles, responsibilities, decision rights of team members
   - What is in/out of scope
   - Deliverables
   - Desired results
   - Detailed work plan
   - Budget

3. **Make sure you take into account the sequencing and timing of strategic initiatives**
   Consider the time of year relative to business cycles so employees can appropriately focus on the project.

4. **Make sure you subject each strategic initiative to project governance and exercise strong project management during implementation**

TOOLS
To ensure you conduct the most comprehensive analysis, use the following tool.

PHASE 3, TOOL 13: PROJECT PRIORITIZATION TEMPLATE
An outgrowth of strategic planning is senior management sponsorship of a number of strategic initiatives. This can be facilitated by using a template that contains all the shortlisted projects and then using a number of objective criteria such as risk level, financial justification, and alignment with the business strategy to prioritize the list.

Directions:
- Column 1: List all of your potential projects.

- Columns 2–5: Work with your finance support person to identify the best criteria to assess the financial viability of each project.
- Column 6: Assess the risk of each project.
- Columns 7–9: Evaluate each project according to the degree to which it supports either your strategies or your key goals.
- Note: Additional decision criteria, including process, technology, organization, and people factors, can be included to round out your analysis. These are typically ancillary and used on an ad hoc basis.
- **Scoring:** The scales vary for each decision criterion. Projects with the highest scores in descending order are the best choices relative to the decision criteria.

	Financial Assessment				**Risk Assessment**	**Strategic Assessment**			**Total Score**
Projects					**Key:** High = 3, Medium = 2, Low = 1	**Key:** High = 3, Medium = 2, Low=1			
						Strategy or Goal 1	Strategy or Goal 2	Strategy or Goal 3	
	ROI	CBA	IRR	Other					

Financial Assessment Key
- **ROI** –return on investment
- **CBA** – cost benefit analysis
- **IRR** – internal rate of review
- Note: These are examples only - Work with your financial partner to select the most appropriate metrics.

PHASE 3, TOOL 14: STRATEGIC INITIATIVES TEMPLATE

This tool is used to put each approved strategic initiative in its correct chronological order to ensure your plans are not excessively front loaded and there are sufficient resources and budget to support success.

This template can be configured in a variety of ways, such as summarizing the strategies with their owners by year. It could include supporting strategic initiatives or even tactics to support each strategy.

It can serve as a useful communication tool, as well as a "sanity check" to ensure your mix of strategies or projects is not excessively front loaded – too many during years one and two and too few in years three through five.

Key Strategies/Initiatives	Owner	Year 1	Year 2	Year 3	Year 4	Year 5
Strategy 1:						
Strategic Initiatives:						
Strategy 2:						
Strategic Initiatives:						
Strategy 3:						
Strategic Initiatives:						

DELIVERABLE

Completing this step will provide the following for use in your overall strategic plan.

D. Completed Charters for Each Strategic Initiative

ACTIVITY 3.6: CREATE RISK-MANAGEMENT PLAN

WHAT IS IT?

A risk-management plan is necessary to proactively identify risks associated with implementing approved strategies and strategic initiatives. The completed plan should identify actions to either eliminate or reduce the impact of each key risk. Once developed it should be updated periodically to reflect changes in the environment.

This activity is commonly completed by facilitating a risk-management workshop. The workshop allows you to rank strategies and projects in terms of two variables: the probability and the impact of risk.

Probability and impact are categorized on a scale of low, medium, and high. Here is a description of that framework:

- Strategies or strategic projects that are high-risk probability and low impact will fall into the "no-go" category
- Strategies or strategic projects that are medium- to high-risk probability and impact fall into the "proceed with caution" category
- Strategies or strategic projects that are low to medium risk with medium to high impact are categorized as "go" projects

The Risk Assessment tool is used to continually assess risk levels as they are implemented. It brings a dynamic feedback mechanism into the planning process; a framework to capture and respond to information about the progress and risk-impact of strategy deployment. It allows executives to take corrective measures if projects are becoming high-risk liabilities, and to ensure that implementation does not stray from the key performance targets defined in the scorecard.

TASKS

Completing the following will help ensure you develop the most comprehensive risk management plan.

1. Collect data to identify risks

Data can be collected using a variety of techniques, including a review of available documentation, surveys, and interviews with key stakeholders and focus groups. Once this data has been tabulated, a risk management workshop should be facilitated to address the most critical risks.

Effective risk management allows you to proactively take actions to reduce or eliminate key risks. Categorize risks such as:

- Legal
- Regulatory
- Competitor
- Technological
- Project management
- Organization/people
- Economic/financial

2. Prioritize risks in terms of probability of occurrence and impact

3. Identify actions to eliminate/reduce "critical few" risks

4. Develop procedures for periodically reviewing the plan. Update the risk plan periodically

TOOLS

To ensure you conduct the most comprehensive risk plan, use the following tool.

PHASE 3, TOOL 15: RISK MANAGEMENT TEMPLATE

Risk mitigation is an important component of strategy execution. This tool can be used to identify risks, assess the probability of occurrence, and determine the impact of each risk on the organization. Risk management should be done at the enterprise-wide and project levels.

Key Risks	Probability of Impact (H, M, L)	Severity of Impact (H, M, L)	Consequences	Response	Owner	Comp. Date
Resources not allocated that were planned or requested (e.g., provide F.T. communications people, employees from Research & Policy for process documentation)	High	High	Reduced buy-in, considerable confusion, reduced confidence in project team	Review overall work plan and recommend resource reallocations. Review resource requirements for each project team and make recommendations to PMO.	R Richards	24 Mar
Critical Path Management not being used	High	High	Possible delays after Day 1, additional resistance	Project plan being updated with more detail. Will focus effort managing work interdependencies between work streams and where critical handoffs are occurring. On a weekly basis PMO will enhance reporting capability regarding monitoring project progress and personnel assignments.	N Thanjan	7 Apr

DELIVERABLES

Completing this step will provide the following for use in your overall strategic plan.

E. Risk Management Plan

ACTIVITY 3.7: CREATE BALANCED SCORECARD

WHAT IS IT?

A balanced scorecard is an integrated set of metrics that can be used to manage the business on a day-to-day basis. The key input for the balanced scorecard is the business plan. In essence, the business plan is translated into a set of leading and lagging measures.

To obtain the full benefit of a balanced scorecard it should be tightly integrated into an organization's compensation practices, recognition process, performance management, and management reporting systems.

The outcomes are of critical importance, but so are the means that generated the outcomes.

TASKS

Completing the following will help ensure you develop the best possible balanced scorecard.

1. Developing a scorecard is an iterative process, so build in a healthy amount of "show and tell" and incorporate the lessons

2. Using the business plan as the primary input, identify and define each category or perspective of measurement

For each perspective, identify 3–5 indicators or types of things you want to measure.

3. Once you have consensus around the indicators, craft one or more

quantitative targets for each indicator

4. Make sure your scorecard is tightly linked to your progress reporting, issue escalation, risk management, and communication activities
Develop a variance-analysis process that will identify the source/cause of performance gaps when actual performance does not meet planned targets.

5. Make sure each employee's performance expectations are tightly aligned with his or her units' scorecard

TOOL
We recommend the use of the following tool at this stage of the process.

PHASE 3, TOOL 16: SCORECARD DESIGN TEMPLATE
Strategy execution can be enhanced by using a set of lagging and predictive measures. This template can be used to think through the detailed aspects of performance measurement, such as the frequency of measurement, how the measure is calculated, who is responsible, and how/where the measures will be posted and used.

Example of Completed Design Template

1. Key Performance Measure: *Return on Assets (ROA)*	**2. KPM Definition:** *The amount of return we are generating from the investment that was made in the site.*
3. Frequency of measurement: *Quarterly*	
4. Formula or computational steps: *Net income / by total assets *100%.*	**5. Definition of computational components:** *1. Net income: The before-tax income produced at Maryland site.* *2. Total assets: Total capital expended to date for Maryland site.*
6. Individual or departments with primary responsibility for update: *Finance*	
7. Baseline performance: *Germany 20xx*	**8. Best practices information:** *TBD - Feb. 20xx*
9. Recommended target performance: *TBD by Finance Manager by June 20xx, must be better than Germany*	

DELIVERABLE

Completing this step will provide the following for use in your overall strategic plan.

F. Updated Enterprise Scorecard

PHASE 4: STRATEGY DEPLOYMENT

PURPOSE

During this phase the approved strategy and supporting initiatives are implemented and communicated across the organization. Unfortunately, many leaders suffer from a convenient form of ADHD. They feel that their job is finished once the plan is complete – the books are distributed and they quickly focus their attention on the next "initiative du jour." Strategy deployment, however, is all about leaders providing visible sponsorship, allocating appropriate resources, and making tough decisions when needed.

Without excellence in execution, even the best-designed plans are doomed to failure. In addition to this leadership blunder, other potential pitfalls include:

- Ineffective program/project management
- Weak leadership/sponsorship
- Lack of attention to contingency planning
- Poor performance reporting/variance analysis

To avoid these derailers, leaders would be wise to support a comprehensive strategy deployment process that includes an initial dissemination strategy, a contingency plan, and cultural alignment efforts to ensure the strategy leverages both the formal and informal organizational infrastructures and networks. Establishing a professional project management office for the deployment can also help ensure a successful rollout.

Figure 6 below illustrates the various activities required for deploying and reviewing the progress on the organization's strategy.

Phase 4: Strategy Deployment

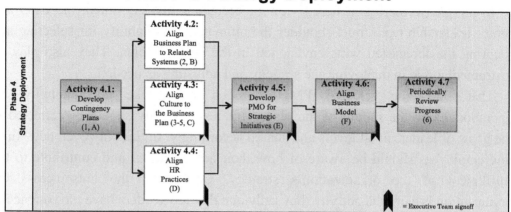

Tools:
1. Contingency Planning Template
2. Strategy 1 Pager
3. Culture Alignment Primer
4. Culture Mapping Template
5. Culture Alignment Template
6. Strategic Project Reporting Template

Deliverables:
A. Contingency Plan
B. Updated Systems/Processes
C. Culture Alignment Plan
D. Modified HR Practices
E. Completed PMO Templates
F. Modified Structure Charts

Figure 6: Strategic Planning 4 – Strategy Deployment

TOOLS AND DELIVERABLES

Figure 6 above depicts the key activities, tools used, and expected deliverables from Phase 4. The key deliverables during this part of the strategic planning process are a contingency plan, a cultural alignment plan, completed PMO templates, and documented modifications to the business/organization structure. To ensure you get the most from your efforts in the deployment phase, keep the following guidelines in mind:

- Strategy deployment is about "organization alignment." The senior team must quickly identify gaps between the current and future architecture needed to deploy the business plan.

- No matter how well you plan, unforeseen things happen. Develop a formal contingency plan with triggers around your major risk factors.

WHO IS ACCOUNTABLE?

In this phase there is a tiered view of accountability. As noted, the CEO and senior leadership team must shoulder the ultimate accountability for selecting and securing the forecasted wins envisioned in the strategic plan. They also play an instrumental role in deploying the strategy and adjusting as needed.

That said, the selected PMO function must take accountability for operationalizing the rollout of the plan. This responsibility should be reflected in the goals of leaders at all levels and shared accordingly. In this way even new, first-line employees should be aware of how their actions affect and contribute to the fulfillment of the organization's strategy. Connecting the dots across the organization is a critical activity, but sadly one that few leaders have the patience to make happen.

ACTIVITY 4.1: DEVELOP CONTINGENCY PLANS

WHAT IS IT?

A contingency plan is a back-up plan to address events that can impact the success of your business strategy. A well-written contingency plan will have identified one or more "triggers" – e.g., if X happens we will respond by doing Y.

Contingency plans should be developed for those scenarios that have the highest probability of occurrence and greatest impact on the organization. The focus should *not* be on "boiling the ocean" and trying to anticipate and address the entire spectrum of potential events.

TASKS

Completing the following will help you develop a comprehensive contingency plan.

1. **Brainstorm a list of "what if" scenarios. Examples are as follows:**
    * What happens if the price of oil dramatically increases?
    * What happens if there is a fire at supplier XXX and production is shut down?

- What happens if supplier XXX forward vertically integrates?

2. Prioritize the scenarios using objective decision filters

3. Develop detailed action plans to respond to the key scenarios

4. Identify triggers that activate each contingency plan
For example:
- If the price of a barrel of oil hits $80, we will switch to cogeneration
- If our supply of XYZ is interrupted we will switch to supplier ABC, where we have already negotiated a contract for emergency capacity at a set price.

TOOLS

We recommend the use of the following tool or its equivalent to help in this regard.

PHASE 4, TOOL 1: CONTINGENCY PLANNING TEMPLATE

The key to using this tool is to not get overwhelmed in detail. Remember that you want to use the "critical few" opportunities and threats identified during phase 1 as the primary inputs. You don't want to solve for the entire realm of possibilities; you want to identify easily recognizable specific scenarios and distinguishable triggers that determine when it is necessary to execute previously developed contingency plans.

Opportunities	Threats	Sample Scenario
A	A	
B	B - e.g., New Technology	**Threat B Happens** XYZ – company develops laser that will zap clots with no adverse risk
C	C	

Action Planner				
Tasks	Start Date	Completion Date	Responsibility	Resources

DELIVERABLES

Completing this step will provide the following for use in your strategic plan.

A. Contingency Plan

ACTIVITY 4.2: ALIGN BUSINESS PLAN TO RELATED SYSTEMS OR PROCESSES

WHAT IS IT?

In order to fully execute your business plan it is imperative to ensure the outputs of the business plan are tightly linked to other related systems such as management reporting, budgeting, etc.

TASKS

Completing the following will help ensure your business plan is aligned to internal systems and processes.

1. Brainstorm and list all of the internal systems/processes that are interdependent with your business planning process

2. Align your balanced scorecard and strategic initiative performance reporting to your management reporting system

This is critical to provide management with a line of sight into strategy execution.

3. Update or develop a process that links budgeting with your business planning process

Make sure this process allocates resources based on the strategic importance of the activity.

4. Develop or align processes for any other interdependent systems (e.g., HR practices such as compensation, performance management, talent acquisition, human capital planning)

TOOLS

We recommend the use of the following tool to help in this regard.

PHASE 4, TOOL 2: STRATEGY 1 PAGER

One of the biggest challenges in strategic planning is fostering understanding of the plan. The strategy 1 pager is a means of translating a full-blown strategic plan into a one- or two-page summary document that can be used to foster cascading commitment throughout the organization. The document should include the strategies, tactics, and key metrics.

Listed below is a completed example of a strategy 1 pager:

Tool Example: Strategy 1 Pager

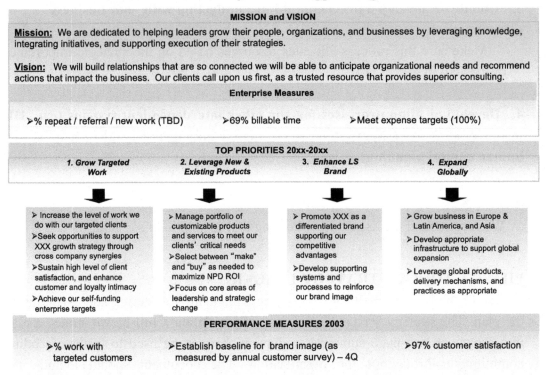

MISSION and VISION

Mission: We are dedicated to helping leaders grow their people, organizations, and businesses by leveraging knowledge, integrating initiatives, and supporting execution of their strategies.

Vision: We will build relationships that are so connected we will be able to anticipate organizational needs and recommend actions that impact the business. Our clients call upon us first, as a trusted resource that provides superior consulting.

Enterprise Measures

➢% repeat / referral / new work (TBD)   ➢69% billable time   ➢Meet expense targets (100%)

TOP PRIORITIES 20xx-20xx

1. Grow Targeted Work	2. Leverage New & Existing Products	3. Enhance LS Brand	4. Expand Globally
➢ Increase the level of work we do with our targeted clients ➢Seek opportunities to support XXX growth strategy through cross company synergies ➢Sustain high level of client satisfaction, and enhance customer and loyalty intimacy ➢Achieve our self-funding enterprise targets	➢ Manage portfolio of customizable products and services to meet our clients' critical needs ➢Select between "make" and "buy" as needed to maximize NPD ROI ➢Focus on core areas of leadership and strategic change	➢ Promote XXX as a differentiated brand supporting our competitive advantages ➢Develop supporting systems and processes to reinforce our brand image	➢ Grow business in Europe & Latin America, and Asia ➢ Develop appropriate infrastructure to support global expansion ➢ Leverage global products, delivery mechanisms, and practices as appropriate

PERFORMANCE MEASURES 2003

➢% work with targeted customers   ➢Establish baseline for brand image (as measured by annual customer survey) – 4Q   ➢97% customer satisfaction

If desired, additional detail can be expressed in a second page that defines specific actions and accountabilities related to the key priorities. As you can see from the sample below, an additional (non-top) priority was added to this view.

Tool Example: Strategy 1 Pager

TOP PRIORITIES 20xx-20xx				
1. Grow Targeted Work	2. Leverage New & Existing Products	3. Develop Consulting Capabilities	4. Enhance Brand	5. Expand Globally

TACTICS 20xx				
1. Define account management accountabilities and metrics; 2. Pilot retainer contract / value added billing (relationship based) 3. Develop financial model (e.g. billable rates, allocation company, contingencies) 4. Redesign time tracking system and link to business analytics	1. Finalize and market an integrated Talent Management process 2. Pilot knowledge networking Community of Practice in Strategic Planning; 3. Develop and communicate leadership/strategic change approach, product, and service summaries 4. Assess NPD possibilities in: executive team development; integration: merger, acquisition and allianceS.	1. Continue to upgrade skills to drive target work, target client goals 2. Determine if new roles should be created as we grow (e.g. specialist) 3. Use monthly lunch and learn sessions for recognition, development, and strategy alignment 4. Implement web-enabled CD 360 and use in development discussions 5. Implement the improved Customer Satisfaction process	1. Develop brand message 2. Assess target customer insights 3. Develop marketing messages, scripts, and tools 4. Execute a communications plan	1. Staff Europe office by Q2 2. Identify targeted stakeholders in Europe and expand business development plan 3. Recommend alternative delivery mechanisms (e.g. website) 4. Form alliances with consulting partners in Europe 5. Update and enhance the Globalization website

SPONSORS				
M. Larson, S. Steves	J. Matthes D. Fairman	N. Harrison, S. Marcum	D. Fairman	S. Evams

DELIVERABLE

Completing this step will provide the following for use in your overall strategic plan:

B. Updated Systems/Processes

ACTIVITY 4.3 ALIGN CULTURE TO BUSINESS PLAN

WHAT IS IT?

An organization's culture is defined as the prevalent cultural characteristics, values, and behaviors held by the majority of the employees.

Aligning culture entails translating the business plan into a number of cultural characteristics and values. These values can then be translated in a small subset of employee behaviors. Once completed, the current culture can be mapped to identify key gaps.

During this activity, we will use our culture alignment model to:

- Identify the types of cultural characteristics, values, and employee behaviors needed to realize the strategy and scorecard.
- Identify specific modifications to the technology, organization, and process architecture to realize the desired cultural characteristics, values, and employee behaviors identified in the previous step.

There are many leverage points in the acculturation process. Examples of culture alignment activities are listed below:

- Onboarding program for new senior and middle managers
- Modifying performance expectations/metrics
- Training and communication for staff
- Replacing leaders
- Modifications to technology, organization, and process architecture to enable the culture to change over time. Specifically, changing business processes, appraisal systems, selection and staffing practices, and reward systems to speed acculturation.

Once the alignment plan has been developed it must be executed. Culture is one of the key gate-limiting factors that can slow down or even stall the implementation of your business plan.

Cultural alignment is an outgrowth of modifying the technology, organization, and process architecture. The plan is expected to:

- Decrease the frequency of undesired cultural characteristics, values, and behaviors
- Enhance the likelihood of desired cultural characteristics, values, and behaviors occurring

TASKS

Completing the following will help ensure your business plan is aligned to the organization's culture.

1. **Facilitate workshop with senior management** to translate business plan into:
   - Future-state cultural characteristics
   - Future-state values
   - Future-state behaviors

2. **Use the culture alignment model**

   Specify five to seven characteristics of culture that are needed to deploy the new business strategy. Examples of cultural characteristics include low bureaucracy, high operational flexibility to respond quickly to market changes, and aggressive use of technology to enable the core processes.

3. **Identify five to ten desired values and their corresponding employee behaviors that are needed to execute the business strategy and scorecard**

   Examples of employee behaviors include willingness to learn new skills, becoming adept at developing and maintaining customer relationships, and demonstrating flexibility regarding task/job assignments.

4. **Map the current culture (use culture mapping tool)**

   This can be accomplished via a pulse survey, focus groups, and interviews. When completed, you can visually identify the difference between the current culture and the future-state culture needed to execute the business plan.

5. **Identify specific changes to the existing technology, organization, and process architecture that are needed to realize the desired cultural characteristics, values, and employee behaviors**

   Pay careful attention to understanding cause and effect. Specifically, what changes need to be made to the technology, organization, and process architectures to either extinguish or enhance specific cultural characteristics, values, and behaviors?

6. **Implement acculturation activities**

   Review management/employee feedback based on questionnaires, surveys, and informal discussions. Use balance scorecard measures as an objective indicator of acculturation effects. Revise your approach as needed.

7. **Periodically evaluate the effectiveness of the modifications**
    Ask the following to help assess the changing situation:
    - Have your actions generated the desired culture, value, and behavior changes?
    - Are there any unanticipated issues?

TOOLS

To ensure your business plan and organizational culture align, use the following tools:

PHASE 4, TOOL 3: CULTURE ALIGNMENT PRIMER

Many books and articles have been written on the topic of culture. Unfortunately the vast majority of these are written from an academic, conceptual, or "touchy-feely" standpoint. The culture alignment primer is a tool that can be used to identify the future-state culture needed to execute the strategy, complete a culture-gap analysis, and identify an actionable plan for evolving culture over time.

Since this tool is very complex we have included detailed instruction on its use.

An organization's culture is defined as the prevalent cultural characteristics (e.g., highly bureaucratic), values, and behaviors held by employees. A **value** (e.g., integrity) shapes our view of reality; what is right or wrong, good or bad. A **behavior** is an observable action that shapes the way people act, react, and operate on a recurring basis. Each value can be broken down into several descriptive behaviors. For example, a behavior that describes the value *integrity* could be: "We believe in complete honesty with each other, even in the most challenging circumstances."

Our collective experience in working with over two hundred companies suggests that culture is a gate-limiting factor regarding the successful deployment of an organization's business strategy. The actions of employees and even stakeholders outside of your organization are influenced by their conscious and subliminal perceptions of the environment. Since your business plan cannot be executed in a vacuum, the existing culture forms the outermost boundaries of what you can realistically accomplish.

Steps to define a culture:

1. Obtain consensus on your organization's business strategy or business plan. In most environments, there is a formal business or strategic planning document. If there is not, you will need to interview key members of the executive team to obtain the information required. **Translate the strategy into three to five strategic thrusts**. (e.g., growth through market expansion in Latin America).

2. Facilitate a structured workshop to identify the **future-state cultural characteristics, values, and employee behaviors** that are critical to be able to successfully execute the strategy. This should either be completed by or heavily involve stakeholders who have a clear understanding of the business plan. This activity is often best completed by a culture-change project team and/or senior leadership.

The following are examples of future-state cultural characteristics needed to execute a business plan:

- Customer focused
- Decentralized decision making/low bureaucracy
- Calculated risk taking

The following are examples of a future-state value and associated behaviors that are needed to execute a business plan:

Passion: We inspire others to take pride in our organization through our dedication to excellence.

Behaviors:
- You do not accept mediocrity in your work or the work of other associates
- You provide critical and actionable feedback
- You are tenacious and driven in the face of adversity

3. Collect data using a variety of sources (e.g., leadership interviews, project team input, culture-mapping pulse survey) and develop an enterprise-wide "as-is" culture map by customizing the cultural dimensions in our culture mapping tool, and a summary of five to ten "as-is" values and their corresponding behaviors. The completed culture map will visually depict where your organization falls along the

continuum of many different cultural characteristics. Note areas of convergence and divergence between the **"as is"** and **"future"** cultural characteristics. Pay careful attention to areas of divergence that are material to successfully deploying your business plan.

At the conclusion of this step, it is necessary to develop a summary of the key cultural characteristics, values, and behaviors that are the most mission-critical gaps. See example below:

Summary of key cultural characteristic, value, and behavior gaps
Key Cultural Characteristic Gaps
- Client focus
- Clarity around strategic direction
- Clarity of roles/decision making
- Centralized decision making
- Leadership alignment
- Too reactive/tactical
- Teamwork

Key Value/Behavior Gaps
Trust:
- You allow people to do their jobs and delegate decision-making authority to the lowest appropriate level.
- You treat people with respect independent of their status.

4. Develop a plan for evolving the culture over time. All organizations, whether they are Fortune 500 conglomerates or small-cap companies, are comprised of three architectures; **technology, organization, and processes**.

We define the **technology architecture** as being comprised of the data employees need to make decisions, the IT hardware, the production/operations technology that is instrumental in delivering your core product/service, and the software applications. The **organization architecture** is comprised of the business systems (e.g., planning, budgeting), management systems (everything from recruiting and rewards to succession planning), the knowledge, skills, and abilities of the workforce, and the organization structure (business model, job design, reporting relationships, staffing levels). The **process architecture** is composed of the business processes; physical layout of work areas; asset base (number, location, type of ownership) of offices, warehouses, etc.; and the administrative policies/business rules that drive behavior.

Although this may appear intuitively obvious, each element of architecture is interdependent. Whenever any part of the architecture is modified it creates ripple effects in the other areas. For example, if a process is modified it will likely impact the IT technology, enabling applications, performance metrics, job design, and physical layout.

Culture is both an output and an input. Culture can be modified over time by identifying the specific cultural characteristics and employee behaviors that are needed to realize the strategy. This serves as a baseline. By modifying the technology, organizational, and process architecture over time you will increase the likelihood that the desired behaviors and cultural characteristics will begin to appear or undesired ones will be extinguished over time.

The visual on the next page provides another illustration of how we can use the template to ensure cultural alignment. Start by identifying five to seven targeted attributes of your business strategy. In this example, it is to increase market share and customer retention. Then ask what type of cultural characteristics and employee behaviors are needed to achieve this strategy. Identify five to seven clear attributes.

Relative to desired cultural characteristics, this can include such things as low bureaucracy, high operational flexibility to respond quickly to market changes, and aggressive use of technology to enable the core processes. Employees must also model the following behaviors: be willing to learn new skills, become adept at developing and maintaining customer relationships, and demonstrate flexibility regarding task/job assignments.

The desired cultural characteristics and employee behaviors will evolve over time if the technology, organization, and process architecture is modified. This would include utilizing relational databases to ensure information is available to lower level personnel. This will lead to decentralized decision making, adopting imaging technology to enhance information availability, reducing the number of layers of management, implementing a skill-based pay reward system, redesigning the physical layout to promote cross-functional teamwork, and reengineering the order entry process.

Crafting and executing a plan of action, paying careful attention to cause and effect, will facilitate culture alignment over a moderate period of time.

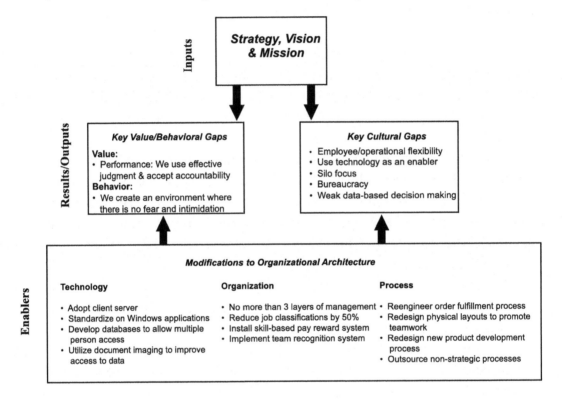

PHASE 4, TOOL 4: CULTURE MAPPING TEMPLATE

This tool draws upon a database of cultural norms we have developed. Before application, it is necessary to customize the map to each organization.

The map can be administered via focus groups or a pulse survey. It is most useful to visually depict the "current" cultural characteristics. Unless an individual is intimately familiar with the business plan, he or she should not be asked to provide input into the future-state cultural characteristics.

Directions: Listed below are a number of cultural dimensions and indices that are organized across a continuum.

- *Step 1:* Review each cultural characteristic and place a **CS** in the column that most closely represents your perception of the **current-state** culture.
- **Step 2:** Place an **FS** in the column that most closely represents your perception of the potential **future-state** culture.
- *Step 3:* Calculate the absolute difference between each culture. The larger the difference, the bigger the culture gap.

Cultural Characteristics	1	2	3	4	Cultural Characteristics	Key Area of Focus
1. STRATEGIC ORIENTATION					**STRATEGIC ORIENTATION**	
Customer/market driven					Technology driven	
Long-term profit orientation					Short term profit orientation	
Employees understand & are committed to strategy					Employees don't understand and/or are not committed to vision/strategy	
Activity focused					Results focused	
Strategically focused					Operationally or crisis focused	
Fast follower regarding product introduction					Leading edge products	
Slow to respond to market dynamics					Flexible, highly market responsive	
2.COMMUNICATION					**COMMUNICATION**	
Top-down focus					Three way	
Infrequent sensing					Frequent sensing	

Cultural Characteristics	1	2	3	4	Cultural Characteristics	Key Area of Focus
Filtered					Open/candid	
3.TRAINING & DEVELOPMENT					**TRAINING & DEVELOPMENT**	
Considerable opportunity for employee development					Limited opportunity for employee development	
Development is based on informal mechanisms with wide degrees of latitude					Development tightly aligned with competency model or career ladder	
Development focuses on current job					Development focuses on current & future job	
4.REWARDS					**REWARDS**	
Focus on rewarding Individual performance					Good balance of individual and team performance rewards	
Employees have minimum involvement in setting performance expectations					Employees have significant involvement in setting performance expectations	
Seniority based					Performance based	
Performance standards are clear					Performance standards are ambiguous	
Compensation at/above market					Compensation below market	

Cultural Characteristics	1	2	3	4	Cultural Characteristics	Key Area of Focus
Employees receive regular performance feedback					Employees don't receive regular performance feedback	
5.DECISION MAKING					**DECISION MAKING**	
Slow					Fast	
Centralized decision making/multiple approval levels					Few approval levels & broad spans of control	
Analytical/cautious					Intuitive/daring	
Authority levels are clearly understood					Confusions exist regarding authority levels	
6.RISK TAKING					**RISK TAKING**	
Risk averse					Calculated risk taking encouraged	
Mistakes are punished					Innovation rewarded	
Management does not solicit or act on employee ideas for improvement					Management encourages and quickly acts on employee ideas for improvement	
7.PLANNING					**PLANNING**	
Short term					Long term	
Reactive					Proactive	

Cultural Characteristics	1	2	3	4	Cultural Characteristics	Key Area of Focus
Informal					Formal	
Intuitive about competition					Constantly monitor competition	
8.TEAMWORK					**TEAMWORK**	
Low cooperation across departments					High cooperation across departments	
Low trust					High trust	
Silo perspective					Process/cross-functional perspective	
Conflict is surfaced and resolved					Culture is polite and conflict is avoided	
9.MGMT. PRACTICES					**MGMT. PRACTICES**	
Leaders hard drivers					Leaders paternalistic	
Policies applied uniformly					Policies applied arbitrarily	
High levels of feedback and coaching					Infrequent or no feedback and coaching	
Few unnecessary procedures, policies, and business rules					Procedures, policies, and business rules used to guide employee behavior	
Cost and control driven					Service and quality driven	
People feel appreciated and valued					People don't feel appreciated and valued	

Cultural Characteristics	1	2	3	4	Cultural Characteristics	Key Area of Focus
Low stress/burnout environment					High workload/long work hours environment	
Workforce embraces change					Workforce strives to maintain status quo	
10. STRUCTURE					**STRUCTURE**	
Roles clearly understood					Considerable role ambiguity	
Organization is flat					Organization has many layers	
11. TECHNOLOGY					**TECHNOLOGY**	
Employees have access to the information they need to be successful					Information is either lacking, untimely, or incorrect	
Technology is not state of the art					Technology is state of the art	

PHASE 4, TOOL 5: CULTURE ALIGNMENT TEMPLATE

This tool helps you pull it all together by articulating the new strategy, vision, and mission; highlighting value, behavioral, and culture-related gaps that could derail your efforts; and noting key technology, organizational, and process-oriented variables to leverage.

The culture-alignment template not only provides a concise summary for senior leaders; it also offers an effective way of sharing this work with the employee population and other stakeholders.

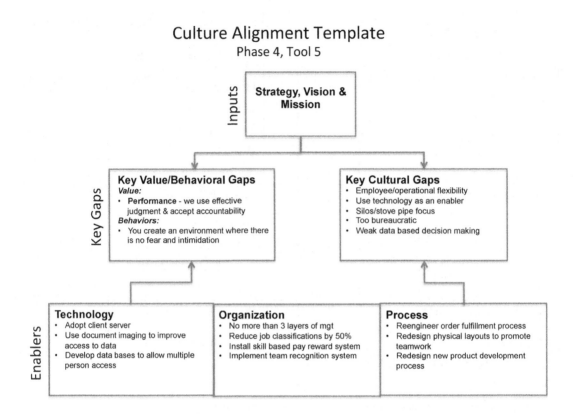

Culture Alignment Template
Phase 4, Tool 5

Inputs

Strategy, Vision & Mission

Key Gaps

Key Value/Behavioral Gaps
Value:
- **Performance** - we use effective judgment & accept accountability
Behaviors:
- You create an environment where there is no fear and intimidation

Key Cultural Gaps
- Employee/operational flexibility
- Use technology as an enabler
- Silos/stove pipe focus
- Too bureaucratic
- Weak data based decision making

Enablers

Technology
- Adopt client server
- Use document imaging to improve access to data
- Develop data bases to allow multiple person access

Organization
- No more than 3 layers of mgt
- Reduce job classifications by 50%
- Install skill based pay reward system
- Implement team recognition system

Process
- Reengineer order fulfillment process
- Redesign physical layouts to promote teamwork
- Redesign new product development process

DELIVERABLE

Completing this step will provide the following for use in your overall strategic plan.

C. Culture Alignment Plan

ACTIVITY 4.4: ALIGN HR PRACTICES

WHAT IS IT?

Depending on the sophistication of your organization and the capabilities of the HR function, this activity may be completed as part of the previous activity. If not, there will be a number of HR practices to review. Some or all of the following may need to be modified to evolve the culture over time.

- Compensation programs
- Talent management
- Benefits
- HRIS infrastructure
- Labor relations practices
- Performance management system
- Recruitment
- Outplacement
- Orientation of new hires
- Diversity / Inclusion

These programs have an immense impact on the culture of the organization and the success of your business plan.

Before reviewing the HR systems, effort should be spent on studying the HR function itself. Is the function traditionally focused (administrative, compliance driven, tactical, and an advocate for employees) or is it a true partner with the line? In the latter case, the HR function is typically both strategic and operationally focused, provides internal consulting support to assist the lines of business in achieving their strategy, and is composed of thought leaders.

TASKS

Completing the following will help ensure your business plan is aligned to your HR practices.

1. Review all HR practices

Expand the list above to include all key programs. While every organization is

different, other common areas of consideration are:
- Employee value proposition
- Special C&B e.g. Executive perks, sales compensation
- Workforce segmentation practices
- Progressive disciplinary/termination procedures
- Labor agreements
- Human capital planning
- Labor relations practices
- Recognition policy

2. **Identify HR practices that conflict with the business plan**

3. **Identify key HR system gaps**

4. **Determine the level of HR practice rationalization that is required**

5. **Develop a high-level plan for completing the rationalization**

TOOLS

Since most organizations have proprietary means or a preferred method of collecting this information, we have not provided a standalone tool for this activity.

We have a number of free resources and white papers at both www.catalystconsultinggroup.org and www.toterhiconsulting.com that provide additional detail on HR best practice. If you'd like more information on how to reshape your organization's HR function please call Catalyst Consulting Group at (860) 518-3583.

DELIVERABLE

Completing this step will provide the following for use in your strategic plan:

D. Modified Human Resource Practices

ACTIVITY 4.5: DEVELOP PMO FOR STRATEGIC INITIATIVES

WHAT IS IT?

A common reason why strategic initiatives often fail is due to poor program/project management. Structure and consistency must be provided regarding appropriate governance, clarity around project teams, and common project-management processes.

TASKS

The following steps will increase the effectiveness of your PMO function.

1. Specify levels of project structure (steering committee, task forces, committees, etc.)

- Select project manager
- Identify sponsoring executive(s)
- Clarify roles/responsibilities/decision-making authority levels
- Select group members

2. Determine toll gates/reviews for the project lifecycle

3. Establish PMO processes such as:

- Risk management
- Issue escalation
- Project portfolio management
- Variance analysis
- Performance reporting
- Cross-team integration

4. Create PMO tools and templates. The key is to ensure the tools are not "overkill." If the project team does not understand the need for specific data requirements, they commonly will not complete the templates. Only request data that are essential and make the templates as user friendly as possible.

5. Provide education/coaching for PMO processes and tools. Many tools are not intuitively obvious to complete. Avoid distributing templates to the project teams without providing appropriate knowledge transfer (e.g., formal training, job aids, completed examples).

TOOLS

Project management is a separate discipline with its own toolkit. We have not provided generic tools for this activity. Custom tools are available upon request. For more information, log on to www.catalystconsultinggroup.org.

DELIVERABLE

Completing this step will provide the following for use in your overall strategic plan:

E. Completed PMO Templates

ACTIVITY 4.6: ALIGN BUSINESS MODEL

WHAT IS IT?

The business model refers to a variety of macro issues concerning how an organization is configured. It includes a number of things, such as what is insourced/outsourced, what is onshored/offshored, and how you go to market (internal sales force, shared sales force, use of distributors).

The organizational structure also needs to be tightly aligned with the business plan and refers to the "shape" of the company. It encompasses issues such as:

- Levels of management
- Spans of control
- Type of structure (functional, product/market, matrix)
- Relationships among functions/divisions (interdependent or not, degree of matrix relationships)

- Reporting patterns, titles, and lines that appear on companies' organizational charts

The review of the structure must be completed in tandem with a review of the physical assets of the organization.

Note: This is one of the more sophisticated activities associated with strategic plan execution. Assign someone who has had considerable experience relative to organization design or use a restructuring methodology to guide you through this process.

TASKS

Completing the following will help ensure you accurately align your business model.

1. Identify how the new strategy will impact the business model and structure.

2. Identify gaps relative the business model and structure.

Note gaps relative to:

- Size
- Spans of control
- Cost structure
- Type of structure
- How interdependent units work together
- How work traverses the organization structure

3. Assess structural fits/misfits independently. Identify:

- Redundancies
- Functionality to centralize or distribute
- Outsourcing opportunities

4. Review and synthesize data: Be sure to collect/analyze structural cost data.

5. Agree on final recommendations for the structure of the new company.

TOOLS

Again, due to the complex nature of this task, we have not provided a generic tool for this activity. Custom tools are available upon request.

DELIVERABLE

Completing this step will provide the following for use in your overall strategic plan:

F. Modified Structure Charts

ACTIVITY 4.7: PERIODICALLY MONITOR PROGRESS

WHAT IS IT?

Depending on the level of competition and the volatility of the markets served, progress should be formally monitored at regular intervals. For organizations operating in highly volatile environments it is not uncommon to have monthly meetings; for other organizations, quarterly meetings will suffice.

The purpose of these meetings is to compare actual versus planned performance, noting where performance variances occur. Root-cause analysis should be conducted to separate symptoms from root causes. It may be necessary to amend your strategy to address unanticipated ripple effects or changes in the marketplace.

TASKS

The following tasks will help you consistently monitor your progress toward achieving the strategic plan.

1. Periodically Review Performance
- Identify the most important data to collect
- Determine what data are already available

- Determine what data you will need to collect and how
- Develop data-collection instruments
- Collect performance data using focus groups, interviews, surveys, review of management reports, feedback from customers, etc.
- Compare baseline metrics with actual performance
- Review company performance reports

2. Identify Variances and Their Sources
- Identify variances
- Categorize variances
  - o **Root cause known** – solution obvious
  - o **Root cause unknown** – additional data needs to be collected

3. Conduct Cause Analysis
- Apply cause analysis tools
- Verify root cause

4. Identify next steps, roles, and timelines

TOOLS

To help manage this ongoing activity we recommend the use of the following tool or its equivalent:

PHASE 4, TOOL 6: STRATEGIC PROJECT REPORTING TEMPLATE

Progress can be reported at an enterprise-wide level, an SBU level, a functional level, and a strategic project level. Depending on the level of assessment the variables need to be customized. For example if you are targeting project reporting you could track a range of variables such as performance to budget or schedule, quality of deliverables, or actual versus planned performance.

Progress reporting is optimized when it is tightly linked to the performance management, compensation, and recognition systems.

Team Name: _____

Report Date: _____

Team Leader: _____

Overall Project Scorecard:

1. Task/Deliverable Status

Legend/Key (G: None; Y: Minor Impact, threaten schedule; R: Major Impact, delay schedule)	Planned Comp. Date	GREEN ●	YELLOW ●	RED ●
Overall Integration Team Schedule				
Key Tasks/Deliverables				
• Task/Deliverable 1				
• Task/Deliverable 2				
• Task/Deliverable 3				
• Task/Deliverable 4				
• Task/Deliverable 5				

2. Synergy Status

Legend/Key (Green: On target to achieve; Yellow: Slightly behind schedule; Red: Significantly behind schedule/in danger of not meeting)	GREEN ●	YELLOW ●	RED ●
Synergy Attainment			
• Synergy/Target 1			
• Synergy/Target 2			
• Synergy/Target 3			
• Synergy/Target 4			
• Synergy/Target 5			

DELIVERABLE

The deliverable for this final stage is simply an ongoing update of the plan. The best strategic plan is the one that is actively used and thoroughly understood by all stakeholders. Use this as your yardstick for measuring the effectiveness of the process.

NEXT STEPS

We hope this book has provided a comprehensive, real-world description of the strategic planning process. We believe that by following the steps outlined in this book, leaders of an organization of any size should be able to research, craft, and deploy a meaningful strategic plan.

We offer associated consulting and training services for complex organizations that may require a more customized approached. If you are interested in help designing your strategic plan, or would like more information on training your internal staff to manage the process, please contact us at:

The Catalyst Consulting Group, LLC
(860) 518-3583
www.catalystconsultinggroup.org

GLOSSARY

Balanced Scorecard
A series of leading and lagging measures that cascade from your business strategy and that can be used to manage the business.

Benchmarking
A process to obtain comparative data in results, resources, and processes from best-practice organizations in order to set and achieve goals.

Best Practice
Widely acknowledged process and/or policy that produces superior results.

Business Analytics
The data that are used to manage the business.

Business Model
A well-designed business model answers the following questions: "Who is the customer?" "What does the customer value?" "How do we make money?" "How we deliver value to the customer at an appropriate cost?"

Business Portfolio Management
The process of reviewing businesses or strategic business units to determine whether they will be your cash cow, harvested, or grown.

Capability Analysis
A structured process for identifying the current capabilities of the TOPS architecture and *internal* strengths and weaknesses of the organization.

Competitive Advantage
Value that a firm is able to create for its customers that exceeds that of the competition.

Contingency Plan
A plan that includes a trigger for addressing an opportunity or threat that has a high likelihood of occurrence and considerable impact on the organization.

Core Process
A process that is critical to achieving the vision and strategy (e.g., new-product development).

Environmental Scan
An analysis of the external opportunities and threats that can impact organizational performance.

Indicator
A label for the category of measurement but not the data (e.g., cycle time).

Initiatives
Strategic projects you intend to implement to achieve your strategy.

Perspectives
Broad categories (e.g., financial, productivity) of measures.

Key Success Factors (KSF)
Those variables that you must excel at in order to achieve your desired vision / strategy.

Lagging Indicator
A desired result.

Leading Indicator
A driver of a desired result, a predictive measurement.

Market Share
The proportion of industry sales of goods or services by a company.

Mission
The defining purpose of an organization (focused on today).

Offerings
The portfolio of all current and future products/services.

Organization Alignment
Aligning an organization's TOPS architecture to closely support its business strategy.

Positioning
What a company wants to be seen as.

Product Portfolio Management
The process used to identify and develop new product introductions as well as manage products through their lifecycle.

Scenario Planning
A structured process that identifies and utilizes trends in the external environment to identify scenarios that can impact organization performance.

Segmentation
Organizing or subdividing the market into similar groupings.

Strategy
Answers the question "What do you intend to do?"

Strategy Development
The "front end" of the strategic planning process that includes the e-scan, internal capabilities analysis, alternative strategy development, and selection of strategic imperatives.

Strategy Deployment
The "rear end" of the strategic planning process, which includes the implementation of the strategic plan and functional strategic execution.

Targeting
Determining which market segments to focus on/avoid.

Target
A quantified level of performance to strive for (e.g., reduce cycle time by 19%).

Trigger
An event (e.g., key supplier goes bankrupt) that identifies when a contingency plan is executed.

Vision
A desired end state in the future that includes big goals and key values.

White Space
The identification of growth opportunities that reflect new areas that the organization has never played in.

ABOUT THE AUTHORS

Ronald J. Recardo is the managing partner of The Catalyst Consulting Group, LLC, a Connecticut firm founded in the early 1990s that helps its clients grow their business, improve their performance, and execute their business strategy. He has more than thirty years of experience as an executive at J&J and Fidelity Investments and as a senior-level consultant for Arthur Andersen. Mr. Recardo has completed projects for more than 130 companies across a range of industries and is the author of seven books and more than fifty articles. He can be reached at rrecardo@catalystconsultinggroup.org.

Tim Toterhi is an organization development professional for a major health-care company based in North Carolina. He began his career in strategic sales in the nuclear industry and transitioned to HR via learning and development. Over the past fifteen years, he has held global roles in change management, leadership development, talent management, and learning operations. He is an executive coach, speaker, and the author of numerous articles on business best practices. He can be reached at tim@toterhiconsulting.com or via www.toterhiconsulting.com.

CPSIA information can be obtained
at www.ICGtesting.com
Printed in the USA
LVOW04s0017010317
525760LV00005B/10/P

9 780986 064661